On My Terms
and Conditions

On My Terms and Conditions

A True Story

RITA S VARMA

PARTRIDGE
A Penguin Random House Company

To order additional copies of this book, contact
Partridge India
000 800 10062 62
orders.india@partridgepublishing.com

www.partridgepublishing.com/india

The true story of Munia's makeover to Aarti. And that of Aarti's transform to the worldly wise Aarti. Of surviving odds to reclaim lost ground to survive strife and supersede supplant surpass and succeed. Not at all costs. But on her terms and on her conditions, industriously.

For her work was worship. Her work had taken her places and would take her forward and further she believed.

The unlettered aimed high with ambition loftier than the learned.

Dedicated to

All women who triumphed against the *odds*.

Dedicated to

Acknowledgement

To Time

To Almighty

To Family

To Aarti

Trailer

This story walked up to me one hazy afternoon. Her timing could not have been better, it was perfect. I had the time to listen to her and she loved to talk, to the extent that if I interrupted her with some of my adventure, she would be visibly annoyed and sometimes had the abruptness to cut me off. Suffice to say she was adorable and a delight to listen too. She was illiterate but illustrated wisdom, she was uneducated but full of knowledge. Ladies and gentlemen I introduce you here to our heroine Aarti.

Slowly, as the days went by listening to her and as I got to know her and appreciate the woman she was, I came to value the fact that she opened up to me instantly, even as I was trying to understand her better. If only I had listened to my mother and learnt to read and write she protested one day. What would you do then I cajoled her, you are leading a good life. I would have written my life story she said simply, raising her eyebrows and stressing on the word life. And, she continued I would put my name and family address at the end of the story. Really, why would you do that I insisted? So that all can know it's a true story, I tell. Does your story have *Masala* I enquired plainly? Yes yes she expostulated glibly, plenty of *Masala* is there. I assured her, taking some pride in myself even though I may have doubted her then, for I said okay then one day I shall write your story. Fine, I'll narrate and you write it, she said. Both of us had merrily laughed off at the idea at the time. We both knew we were both saying what we were saying for the sake of saying. We were both sizing up each other at that stage.

I was reminded of the time, years ago in the tiny town of Lonavala. There one day, as the sun shone up after days of lashing rain, my neighbour and I got talking across the hedge. The clouds and the mist had evaporated, so the Duke's Nose, the vertical hillock at some distance was detectable after long. We were young and gregarious then. She had stitched a nice frock for her daughter, while complimenting her I mentioned that she could perhaps have done this like that, suggesting an alteration. Impressed she said, you know I can stitch but cannot imagine the patterns. And I can imagine the patterns but place a sewing machine before me and I will run faster than a sprinter. We had both laughed out loud then, agreeing on a joint venture. Traversing through life we do come across people we take instant liking to. We consider things together, while we know in our hearts we shall never endeavour them. But at that moment, when they occurred we were both really committed. It's just that the school bus had arrived then and the children had taken preference. The venture lost amidst the mist. Such things happen to all of us. So when it happened again I did not place much value to it nor did Aarti.

But casually she started spending more time with me, mostly narrating her day and generally lounging around. That was when she started impressing me and talking to me in great detail. Sometimes on purpose I would ask her to relate some of the incident again to my daughter's as I tallied the occurrence with her initial narration. I was completely wrong in my assessment of her, her story did not have *Masala* but it was liberally sprinkled with *Garam*

Masala – spicy hot and sour. I did consider then to name the working title - spicy hot and sour. But the moment I typed them they occurred to resemble 'sunshine mist and the rainbow' and immediately my creative skills came to the fore with a warning, the yellow triangle with an exclamation mark, and denied it vehemently. Darn I wondered do I have any liberty here or am I just to labour as per the desires of the artistic.

She was a workaholic. She would be like a pundit without his vedas if she was without some. She preferred instant appreciation on accomplishment of a task was very evident. For if one overlooked to do so she would ask for a response. To anyone's delight all work would be done with utmost diligence. She was fiery she was flamboyant.

Very early on in her life she established the fact that her conditions were grim and gloomy. She may be born into severe conditions but she vowed not to die in a state of whimper. *Rote hue aate hain sab hasta hua jo jayega.* (everyone arrives into this world crying but the one who shall depart from it smiling.) I suggested, she chuckled yes yes what a nice film. There was this dance Rekha had in the film. Now I am used to everyone across the board gush about Amitabh Bachchan when the superhit film Muqqadar ka Sikandar is mentioned. And she was so devoted to her choice of Rekha ji it pleased the writer in me. She was not a stereotype.

First Half

That Munia as a young Aarti was known was going to lead a dramatic life was evident to her mother even before she learnt to utter the famous words maa-mother. For as a toddler she had her father stand behind the open wooden cage of the courts, on charges. Her mother recounted this to her.

Her father Babu as he was called by his children owned and ran a cycle repair shop. Eerie and very very peculiar I wondered. So would some of my readers, for my first novel had Sayyed owning and running a cycle repair shop too. That was imaginative this was for real. When those words were inventively written I had not set eyes on Aarti nor was she anywhere close-by. Could Aarti somehow be in the know of my manuscript which was in its final stages of print? Could some of my notes have made their way to her I wondered. She was unread unlettered but was clever ambitious and honed the knife blade of her instincts of survival on the stone of time. That is when it dawned, why I was unnecessarily stressing over fiction.

This brought me to another scenario. What if she were to accuse me of say plagiarising? For soon enough every now and then some very subtle semblance and similitude seemed to suggest it-self and sprinkle it-self as we proceed and be detectable to the most discerning reader. And therein lay the essence of beauty of this tale. Not exactly a déjà vu kind of a feeling but the merging of miniscule facts with the fiction can be felt throughout. Fiction it seems to me is born out of the writer-author. So in that sense it's totally correct to say that some of the parent's expressions and experiences are bound to seep into or slip by either noticed or unnoticed into the hard-bound. The pearls that are strung together to get the sum total of any writer shall definitely have some of the beads that are bound to showcase themselves in the writings.

This also led me to reflect about why in the first place I had based my character Sayyed such. Early influences, was the answer I received on juggling my feelings. My school bus arrived at the stop early so we could reach school 15 km away at Sadar Jabalpur, in time. We were just two of us. My elder sister and me and Laakhan Singh my father's trusted peon who escorted us to the bus stop. Apart from us was the sole cycle repairman under the huge tree, who tended to early morning commuters to the Gun Carriage Factory on one hand and the Ordnance factory on the other. Both names self evident of the product manufactured therein. Government Engineering College colony, the colony we resided in lay someplace in between the two factories. He was a very systematic man with neatly lined tools, glue that smelled divine, emery board that resembled the school blackboard duster, a pail filled with water a trunk in which he stored the spare-parts and of course the air pump strategically placed and leaning on a stand.

Oh yes be assured I did try my hands on the pump and after the initial free-flowing attempts the pressure became unmanageable for me. We were skinny sisters. You need to eat more Laakhan Singh would prod. So this was how the character of Sayyed was born. Strange, that I had not given it so much thought during its conceptualisation. Also it was no wonder that Sayyed set up shop at Sadar Bazaar in Delhi. It was also no wonder that the gate, on which the children took turns to swing-on in my first-written, was the colony gate on which we swung as we awaited for the bus to arrive.

She was born into a large balanced family, consisting of 6 brothers and 6 sisters. She stood at number 8 if one counted from the eldest with 4 siblings younger to her. One day while she was divulging her hearts contents out, I questioned her on what was her very earliest of thoughts and remembrances? Taken aback by my interruption she visibly adjusted her thoughts from the barge of her convey. She was quick to supplement within moments, give her the bait and she would always fall for it, such a dear she is I never failed to appreciate the fact. But her haphazard thoughts had to be curbed and curtailed when they became a hazard to the narration. One can safely say that if the writer's block is a writer's fear then the raving protagonist her / his trepidation.

Like the popular news-reader Arnab Goswami she hesitated just for that minimalistic moment and uttered *Rekha ke jaise banne ka showk tha*. Well, all my life expectations went for a loss or were it better to say that they went for a huge toss. Now who can, how can, you I or anyone, think of a person who can claim that their very early memories was craving to be like Rekha? I did not want ambiguity in her tale so I quizzed her sharply, are you watching any Tv serials soaps or films and getting inspired by them? Aree no, she said a little surprised a little offended. I left it at that but made a mental note that the query needs to addressed again, maybe she did not get me right maybe she wanted to impress with her tale maybe she thought her answer would impact the reader.

But I was not going to let go, off the hook, my treasured catch of the day too. So a little later I prodded her back to the topic of Rekha ji. You wanted to imitate Rekha, fine what next? Next I wondered what is to be done what can be done to be like her, she supplemented pleased as a punch. Fashion, retorted her intelligence. Paisa (money), shall be needed for doing fashion, realized her little mind. How will this paisa come? It reasoned. Paisa will come from work. It responded. Some work needs to be done. It reckoned logically.

When she went to school she was exposed to the vagaries of life, of the classes in schools, of the classes in society. When a classmate came to class wearing spanking new round earrings she commented to her friend, let it be I shall get them too, when I work I shall get them too. What perfect genes her parents had passed on to her I awed. Never did the thought of acquiring paisa by other means corrupt her persona. When this paragraph was being written on Microsoft Word document I asked her if she was ever spanked by? Oh yes she agreed unabashedly. Trust all schools and mother's to do that as a common component of an intricate and integral syllabus of grooming their brood, those days.

School was not the place of my choice. I wanted to be free and roam the world, I mean city she corrects, which was my world until then. I could be very spoilt; *badtameez* was the word she used. Those days I was known as Munia and my younger brother Munna. I loved and thrived on mischief he abhorred studies. Together we were a team. Life was simple life was fun. We lived each carefree day in merriment. We put our tiny brains together to overcome any obstacle and obstinate behaviour that came our way. We were the rulers we were ruling.

7

Well mostly until the day the newly appointed female teacher crossed our path and daggers. She did the undoable, she picked up the mustard yellow wooden ruler with black symmetric markings from its end, raised her arm till it was in line with her head, similar in approach to the dacoit shown taking pledges in films and before I knew it she was holding the palm of my right hand. At that very instance, a blinding thought entered my mind and immediately I shrug my fist off her rough hand. The ruler whooshed past my ears and unable to be contained midway in its path by my outstretched palm, it continued its downward journey unabashedly, till it was facing the floor. The class sat transformed and transfixed at the unthinkable blunder committed by me, aghast and speechless but a tiny voice escaped from the one in wonderment at my boldness in the face of terror.

The moment this sound wave approached her ear she was incensed and infuriated manifold by the chuckle, furious at the thought of tarnish to her tough image being crumbled at the very onset, of a staffroom stares of pity, of living a limp-less listless life of a wounded tigress in the circus called school, she collected her whims about her and the small left wrist with the extended open palm, triumphantly the wood was stroking it stridently. Aghast I looked at her and then at the bruise in the process of transforming from red to purple to black and finally settling for blue, over my lifeline. It was a live demonstration of and a perfect example of being beaten black and blue. Some of the classmates muffled their mirth and amusement, but one back bencher covered her mouth modulated her voice and chuckled 'proper'.

The cochlea or the ear is an auditory system. It also aids to balance the body position. So, they are symmetrically placed on the opposite sides of the skull close to the brain the source of imbalance. The journey from the ear lobe to the brain lobe is simply magnificent. Sound waves received and focused by the outer ears are transmitted to the inner where they are modulated. The inner ear is filled with liquid and consists of the hair-cell receptors that release chemical neurotransmitters when stimulated. Sprinkle in some more complex electronics and information safely reaches the temporal lobe of the brain where it is registered as sound. The audio range or the bandwidth for the human ear lies within the range of 20 Hertz to 20 Kilohertz. Hertz is the current unit of frequency, which replaced the previous unit of cycles per second commonly called cps and is named after the German physicist Heinrich Hertz for his contributions in the field of electromagnetism. Btw current here is not to be confused with current in amperes - the electrical charge carrier.

If hearing was the chief function of the ear then affording balance when stationary or mobile is its crucial purpose. In addition the innocuous ear assists two further types of balances. Static balance permits one to experience gravity and dynamic balance which allows for feeling of acceleration. Spoken simply this meant the downward pull and the forward thrust or the force felt vertically and the force felt horizontally. Basically, it implied the pulling down and the pushing ahead. Clearly the sound from the cheeky kid unbalanced the newly appointed teacher when the audio hit her brain nerves. Which of the two hits was mightier would be known later on when the resound would reverberate along the corridors in daylight and in her minds passage at nights.

Munna and Munia took the incident badly too. Their reputation was also at stake. If they did not manage to avenge shortly, their existence as prime movers of the class would cascade to a mediocre level before long. They hatched a plan to get even, arriving early they sneaked in from the side entrance, they collected the saw-dust from the chalk box. Placed a bench over the table and then another bench was balanced over it precariously to just about manage to reach the fan blades when she stood on her raised toes. Quickly the wood splinter was placed on each of the three rusty blades. She stepped down the topmost bench then jumped down to the stone floor in great enthusiasm. Rearranging the furniture they scooted in a hurry with glee writ large on their faces.

It was decided that she would report to school a little late that day, to ensure that she was not to be blamed for the fiasco in any case or matter. She bunked the morning prayers during assembly and also the attendance roll-call. But as luck would have it she stuttered in at the very precise moment when the teacher asked a student to switch on the fan. Nothing happened for a few moments as the blades took to swirling reluctantly after remaining stationary during the long hours of the evening and night. The tutor looked at its wobbly gait when the fan began rotating with a noisy jerk and made a mental note to inform the administrator that this fan needs to be checked by an electrician for a faulty capacitor, fans in most classrooms were in urgent need of lubrication if not a fresh coat of paint too she sighed. She even knew that he would show his haplessness at the non availability of funds.

At that precise moment it happened. Some of the coarse wood shavings crushed to dust dispersed uniformly over the uniformed but most of it circulated and scattered over the target in question. Her head was bent low over the book, when dust began to settle over her register she looked up in dazzled amazement. Munia, rang the bells of her mind and every pore attested the fact. That slimy creature needs to be shown her place. It was faceoff time. The dust was strewn over her clothes smudging her eyes cascading over her long eyebrows and settling like snowflake, amassing over her hair.

Her prime accused stood at the doorway portraying a sorry figure concealing her victory cry triumph written largely in her eyes. She stood there her hand raised, asking for permission to be granted to enter the classroom. There was not an iota of doubt in anyone's mind that she had outstanding abilities. They had hatched a great plan. They had succeeded at it with greater élan. She had calculated well. Though the laws of physics were unknown to her and would remain to be so for life she had reckoned well the forces of gravity and centrifugal.

This was not the first instance when she had taken on the mighty teachers. When she started attending school not at the stipulated age of five but six, she was very keen on attending classes like her elder sister's and brother's, of becoming proud owners of copies pencil and a school bag, of learning. After her eldest sister Parvati was married the family fell on bad times she insisted.

Hence the new entrant to school was deprived of the better school closer to home and the schoolbag too. She was sent along with Munna to the government run school at some distance with the handed down schoolbag of her sister, at age six so she could accompany her brother Munna aged five. My father's pride had begun to crumble in front of our very eyes since the marriage. It was just the beginning, for the entire row of children stood before him to be married and settled off.

All her enthusiasm was replaced with dullness by the change of plans. Unfortunate said her brother's in tease. Unfortunate and me she retaliated, no way let's see who is unfortunate she said hurt, she hardly understood the meaning of the word. But she knew by the tone that it was a bad thing that had happened to her such that her siblings felt sorry for her.

Defiant she approached the gates of the school that was responsible for all the misery in her life. Disobedient was to become her middle name. Lessons available free for learning she did not learn. Alphabets number counting rhymes she knew them all by heart but when asked she remained tongue tied. Until her attitude incensed a teacher much. She called her to come and recount the counting. Stubbornly she stood in front of the class noncommittal; the enraged teacher slapped her on her shoulder fuming at all her efforts being brought to naught.

She had done the unpardonable mistake in Munia's eyes. Human Rights would enforce that slapping was a crime much later somewhere late in the twentieth century; she was the one who knew a wrong from a right by instinct. She reasoned that if her mother got to know of this harsh action by her teacher she would fight tooth and nail on her behalf. But the hurt on her back was not of great proportion so little Munia beat herself up and landed in front of her mother bruised. One look at her and her motherly instincts came to the fore as ably perceived by her daughter.

Next day early morning the distressed mother accompanied her girl to school and challenged the teacher in question to never ever, as much as touch her daughter again. It's my prerogative but I refrain from hitting her as much as I can. But none can dare touch her. So your mother did spank you? Unruly needs to be curbed I now know that on becoming a parent. Do you remember any or maybe the first incident of being unruly? She was reminded of the following incident.

Culturally the spring festival Holi is synonym to colour carnival celebration, where friends family familiar foreigner bond and have fun with coloured powder and water. Traditionally Holi is a signification of the victory of good over evil by perishing thy vices, within and without, into the rising flames of the Holika, the bonfire burnt at community centres with much fanfare. Lore says demon king Hirankayshap's sister Holika took his son Prahlad into the pyre fire to blaze him. Holika who was blessed with the boon of the shawl the *dushala* that would shield the one who wore it around them, was ironically burnt. The stole unwrapped from her shoulders just as a freak wind blew across an arid day and wrapped itself around the boy. While Prahlad a profound devotee was saved by his Lord Vishnu the Preserver the Protector, his villous and devious aunt was burnt. Holi is derived from Holika. So in that sense its triumph of the Lord's blessings and swift justice, of love and forgiveness too in modern times.

During her childhood in her parents' home the festival did not come to mean any of the above for her. Mischievous minds are full of wayward ideas to celebrate the day, in good humour. Her father had taken a small loan from the Lala for the occasion so that the children could enjoy the day as deemed to merit the cheerful festival. Like always he would work till late and redeem his pride later. He handed the token amount to his wife who chipped in some rupees that she had hidden at the bottom of the brass container that she used to store rice.

Money could ward off most problems she had learnt as a child bride. For when her mother in law was grievously ill, her mother lamented why we don't call for the learned *vaid* the practitioner who cures her of fever. After hesitatingly taking due permission from her father in law, her visiting father had called for the *vaid* who was consulted. His prescribed medicines seemed to work for her but the second batch of pills could not be procured. She had known then that money was bigger than the *vaid* or medicines.

How or from where she made those soiled notes materialize he knew not, nor did he question her. Like most housewives she pinched a few paisa here a few there from her daily expenses. She bargained hard. And in her case she would collect and cooked the *chowlai ki bhaji* the feral uncultivated vegetable that grew in the wild on her return each day. Exotic common market vegetable was cooked for festivities only. Festivals occur with great reluctance on one's Timeline to spread joy and cheer, so they must be humbly revered and one must rejoice in the revelry by following tradition, food preparation decorum and decoration she would sermon.

Munia and her gang would gear up early in the morning by oiling their hair so that the colours did not settle on their scalp and wore spotless dresses they could shun after the festival. Whereas most festivals are associated with purchase of and wearing of bright new dresses this perhaps is the only celebration world over where old clothes are worn with flair. Seldom have one seen any with new attire on this day. Only one occurrence she remembered when a newly married groom was bringing home his wedded wife and the occasion demanded he wear his best clothes. He was also not spared by the neighbourhood children who swarmed about the bride singing *bhabhi aayi bhabhi aayi,* sister in law has arrived sister in law has arrived as they coloured his new blue long shirt. He did scold them in mock anger but a happy man allows for all mischief on a happy date.

The boys wore colourful topi's available for the occasion. They would go house hopping, visiting friends and family to play with colours and eat the savouries and sweets on offer. Since they could not afford to spend a large sum on colours she and her younger brothers would soak the seeds of Tukmalanga overnight. The next day these kernels would exudate thick copious mucilage. When the colourful Holi got over, when they finished all the *abeer gulal* (the coloured powder) the rowdy and motley group of youngsters switched to playing with this gluey substance.

Every now and then I would slip homeward plunge my dark gummy fists into the sweets jar and scoot away. When my mother saw the sweets and other foodstuff being spoilt such, she raised a hue and cry. Not finding any of the children around she homed on to her father who sat on a chair by the doorway rejoicing in the children's celebration. Why don't you prevent the boy's and girls from messing up the food stuff? He let her complain go astray. But when she demanded he just smiled at her and trying to pacify her spoke indulgently let the children soak in the festivities, my dear. His wife of many years hurriedly shied away like a new bride on listening to the loud words of endearment, but not before issuing the warning that he keep the erring child at bay. Both husband and wife knew that her words had fallen on deaf ears, for togetherness in years is the breeding ground for familiarity with clarity. He was not sure how long he could afford the children with their joy.

Do you get it now, why do I spank you such? But lord Shankarji pardon me the girl incenses me irritates me and infuriates me much on a pious day like Holi. Spare me lord and spare the child. All this holy drama she performed after all the thrashing was done with, concluded Munia mischievously. Spare the rod and spoil the child, her village born and brought up mother sure went by the adage.

But the slaps could not deter her. She was back with the gang enjoying the day to the hilt. They would stand hidden from the passerby and when anyone whosoever he may be approached they charged at him, placed the blob of the gummy on his hair and fled before their now unrecognisable faces could be recognised. Such fun such joy these actions offered, the children of today know not. It would be only later in the eighties after the Amitabh Bachchan Jaya Bhaduri Sanjeev Kumar Rekha starred song *rang barse bheege chunarwali rang barse...* would become a cult song, that men and womenfolk are now seen donning crispy whites on Holi.

Tukhmalanga and Chia seeds have similar characteristics but as the name suggests they are derived from different botanical sources. When these seeds are soaked overnight in water both are known to ooze thick copious mucilage. Whereas Chia seed have been found to possess great nutritional value, tukhmalanga finds usage as a medicinal herb. It's the best medicine for treating boils and ulcer suggests our protagonist. Place the seeds and wrap a bandage around it and sure enough by next day the boil would have erupted of the entire puss thereby healing the wound. It's a much prescribed tonic in Unani Tibb. It is said to have cooling effect too, so in summers it's the much added additive to ice creams. Tukmalanga seeds are also known as tukmaria, saja seeds or tukhmaria seeds. These are called sweet basil seeds too. There are many health benefits of using tukmalanga seed in our food.

The gardener's wife *malin* as she was universally dubbed was on the lookout for school going kids who did not want to attend class. She indulged them to come and assist her. Child labour is cost effective for her retail she had reckoned. Educationists rightly say that child labour deprives the child of childhood among other aspects. The law of our land suggests that any child below the age of 14 cannot be employed by any. According to International Labour Organisation this age is fixed at 15. But the lady was ignorant of the laws both inland or the international or the offence she was involved in unknowingly. Nor did the policeman on duty know of any of it else he would surely have benefitted by some amount from the children's earnings. The lady was very clear when it came to her business and charity did not mingle with it. She was earning to keep the fires of her home burning and not to regale. This was her comment when relatives or clients insisted on some extra flowers.

Some from weaker sections some weak in performance came to her on their own accord. They made ten packets of flowers and deliver them to her patrons; in turn she gave them 4 annas. She operated from the vicinity of the Khedapati temple close to her school. Young Munia became adept at selecting the flowers and some Tulsi leaves and packing them in the A4 size newspaper. Quickly she would roll it to form a loose cone shape, then the top free end was folded secure such that the flowers remain unblemished. These were delivered to the residents nearby for their morning prayers or evening *aarti*. Soon she was earning more than the rest. The math she learned here was far more interesting and advanced than that taught in the rooms without practical application and appreciation.

During festivals and holidays she asked them to string one kilo *genda* flower garlands for one rupiya. Rupee rupiya rupaiyya rupay all units of the currency in English and Hindi. Munia her best apprentice and her darling earned *ek chavanni* that is to say a quarter of a rupee extra, for she accomplished much more than the rest who either shammed or struggled with the entangled garlands. All errands were priced; the packets containing loose flowers were to be delivered but the garland was sold at the temple venue itself. She remembered the festival fair of Basant Panchmi the fifth day of spring, when *malin* would ask them to fill the small earthen pots with soil and stick two sticks of the brightly yellow or saffron *genda* flower and one stem of a leafy twig. These were delivered to her patrons as well as sold at the temple fair. Marigold known as *genda* was available through the year in varied hues and sizes.

Fashion and bangles she could now purchase from the vendor who brought his ware in a glass covered rectangular suitcase. Maroon and red bangles red lipstick, she wished to have long hair like the cine-star she came to copy from the newsprint. So she purchased streams of black colour ribbon entwined it to her plait and let the ends fall long and loose to duplicate her favourite, whose name was unknown to her then. She was clever enough to rub off all her makeup before her mother's arrival from the fields. One day her mother spotted her stuff. She enquired all her children when all refused she complained to her husband. Angered she took the stuff and threw it out. When the neighbour washer man's daughter Beheni saw the commotion she chipped in *arre mausi* (o aunt) these bangles belong to Munia. This piece of information enraged her more. Unknown to her she was following on the lines of the lines penned by – Sahir Ludhianvi

jahan sach naa chale wahaan jhoothh sahee.
sukh dhoondh le sukh aparaadh naheen.

Speaking or telling white lies to circumvent unpleasantness was fine. But when the general became a major, when one spoke of principal's truth and only truth matters, she was to learn later.

Doing fashion was her sole purpose until then. Her mother may have stopped her from doing so, by flinging her bindi bangles and other cosmetics into the open drain. But young Munia's pursuit for dolling up remained intact and could not be tossed. She would get up late at night when all were asleep and craft numerous slender plaits or colour her eyes patiently. Then prance about and pout around gleefully.

Once her elder brother saw her on one of her spree and followed her, when she was on her delivery rounds and reported that she was running errands for *malin chachi*. Mother went to school the next morning and came to know of her mischief. That, of Munia who would keep her school bag in class and disappear. She would come back again when the long school bell indicating end of school rang, pick up her tattered bag and stand in queue to collect her portion of the allotted *churma* and return home. Schools provided its pupil with roasted wheat flour *panjiri* and biscuits to lure

19

the children to school as well as assist in keeping the health of the budding students in prime condition. She threatened *malin* with dire consequences if she were to learn of her daughter bunking books in favour of flowers. Her mother found the act belittling.

Initially the ayah at the school gate would not allow her out so Munia learnt to tease her *badi aayi maharaani* o mighty queen, incensed by her tease she came after her but young Munia was too quick for her for she would dodge her and toss her food or sneak out when she was inattentive or running some errand for the principal of Leelawati charity school. The old lady could not leave her post at the gates of the school nor bear to see her lunch scattered by the brat brute every day. If they can't check her and keep her in the class it's their fault she reasoned and morally absolved herself from the trespassing little monster.

My school is still operational she declared with pride and has become more affluent. Earlier there was no formal uniform in use. Some children did wear uniforms of their parent's choice but we wore normal dress to school and it made bunking easy for me. We sat on woven jute strips called *taat ki patti* in row's during the initial years as there was no furniture provided for the new beginners initiating and inducted to school. They used *khadiya* to write, on the slate with handle to hold it. These *khadiya* lumps were powdered and a sleek pencil-like stick fashioned from bamboo stalk with a sharpened end was used to write. The sharp nib-like end was dipped in the powder for normal purpose. When the teacher conducted tests she asked us to wet the powder so that when we stacked up the slates the writings remain intact. Next year onwards we used alabaster - the fine textured white colour hard gypsum sticks for writing on slates. The year after that benches and desk was to be a huge initiative for all.

When she did not learn her lessons diligently her teacher would place the sleek bamboo stick between her fingers and twist her knuckles about it. Insinuating she learn her lessons properly. When the pain became unbearable she would hastily agree to her teacher. But the next day would be another day of mischief and fun at school.

I do not send you all the way to school to become a wayward child; she expressed grief as she pulled Munia by her ear. What is to become of this child of mine she lamented aloud who bamboozles right under my nose? Henceforth you shall not attend any school-wool she declared with finality. On my terms Munia sighed to herself, did not I say so to my brothers when they taunted at me calling me unfortunate? Young Munia had by the time turned into a fully fledged rebellion. Hence when asked not to attend school now, she would on some pretext or the other, find her way to the institution, albeit for other reasons.

Firstly, there was the lure of money. Secondly, her commitment to *malin* was to be honoured at all cost. Thirdly when her over burdened mother could not take her fooling around any longer she would admonished her strictly by restricting her to a room and on occasions tried to curb her misbehaviour by not giving her, her supper. An enraged hungry Munia would then go to school she was still enrolled to and now plead with the same ayah at the main gates to allow her to be led in. 'Twist of fate' the ayah would say to this unruly student and satiate her fallen pride. As Munia was to say later Ma Vidya, the mother of knowledge was not with her so how she could have studied without her consent. In actuality she by all means meant Ma Saraswati, the goddess of knowledge music and learning's.

She rightly refrained to put forth her plea to the goddess Ma Saraswati and tagged only onto the fraction of the whole, Ma Vidya (goddess mother of knowledge). For life is the greatest teacher and Ma Saraswati did expose her to the learning's that the pages and written words cannot attempt to match. Also music can be acquired if one is a keen listener having melody inclined ears. But the three R's as they were popularly known would remain abandon if Reading (w) Riting and (a)Rithmetic were to be discarded.

One must say those days of tomfoolery were the best. To while away my time with friends we would play with the tiny hard fruit of the eucalyptus tree. Spin them by swirling them between my thumb and forefinger and leave it on the sand to twirl. See which of them toppled last and the patterns they created. Make tiny slashes on the bark of this tree and then collect the oozed and dried gum after a few days. Soak these brown shiny beads in water and add torn strips of paper. Leave this mess till most of the water evaporated and then fashion cups saucers dolls and animals from this mashed up recycled dough. Yes, she was referring to a crude form of papier Mache.

They would accompany their mother to Ghoshiana the milkman's *chatta*, the compound where he tied his cows and buffalos. We would collect the cow dung and assist mother in making cow dung cakes called *kanda* used like firewood for cooking. When they prepared 500 kandas they got to take 250 home. Her mother would sell these to the families at the cost of 40 rupees for 100 pieces. This way they survived when her father fell ill and when he hurt his eye from the splintered nut that flung at him on securing it too tight. With her help he was able to repay the loan slowly but steadily and over a period of time.

Her elder brother Ramakishen was not much into studies and began spending time with friends. He did not learn to assist at home. He was lured by politics and began spending his days at the local politicians (*neta's*) place and loved to stay with them. When Kiran Bedi was posted there she was the talk of the town she asserts, diverting from her narration. Her brother had become a favourite lackey of the *neta* she informs. Her other brother did not study much after she left school nor learnt any skills just played the local game of gilli danda all day and loitered around.

I may have many children but none are for adoption my mother growled at the lady's dare. How dare you come to me with such a bizarre wish? The wise woman then diluted her stand by saying let your daughter come to me for a while. I shall feed her and take good care of her.

Mother fell ill as she was expecting again. That was when all hell broke loose. That is when the family troubles started in earnest. The axle around which the family revolved automatically experienced some obstacle in their path. The smoothness of the drive was further interrupted as her grandparents grew infirm with ageing. Her aunt's were now all married and gone, some far some near. Her uncle's now married too were involved in their own. Mother's illness did not allow for her to go for preparing cow-dung cake. This continuous source of bringing in the resourceful resource money was suddenly terminated.

Now younger brother's Bhalla and Pupoo left their studies mid-way and joined the garage of a muslim uncle *chachoo*. They began bringing money home and worked hard. Pupoo learnt to drive as well and with their salary and savings we could purchase a buffalo. Father felt assured of his sons.

Nine months passed by and her new sister arrived. The brothers celebrated much her arrival. After the pooja on the fifth day mother rested for 3 more days and on the 8th day she was back to her work of making *kanda*. Some women are born with great tensile strength, the maximum stress a material can withstands before failing and before falling apart. They were all growing up fast; the family was expanding in two's and four's, similar to the process of fission. They needed to be fed a good diet she argued with her father who submitted to her plea calmly. He understood well this promulgate postulated by his own dear mother. When his young wife arrived at his home his mother pleaded and prodded with his young child bride to his amusement, to eat well so she could look after her family suitably she would cajole. His mother would boil peas and chick peas for her and feed her by using a long twig as fork. Her words were etched on her tender mind, as the most sacred privilege to be borne by a housewife.

When her sons, now strong and hardworking admonished her saying she stay home she smiled at their affection for her. It does not take a long time for fortunes to turn, she explained them. Just as much time as is called for to blink the eyelids and the picturesque could turn to piqued, she wished for them to hone this lesson well. She a village woman by birth knew this message too well. Her mother in law had left them one day, satisfied she had groomed her progeny, but Mahadei could not bear the suddenness of her vacancy, her heart still ached for her. She never could adjust herself to the fact that life could leave one in the lurch.

Keeping aside this thought that grieved her much she would shift gears to the present reluctantly. They needed to wed the girls she protested with her brothers. The mention of this duty considered a responsibility by all male members quietened them always. If one were to ask her what wish she would ask for, if she was given a boon by the god's she would ask for time to sit. To plainly sit down relaxed for a moment without thought care or concern. To bring back the days she spent with her caring mother in law, whom she continued to miss much for she did not remember much of her own mother.

Words that never left her heart to rise up and reached her lips, words she never uttered were well acknowledged by her husband in a silent pact. His mother had tutored her as her own and the pupil had learnt with a keen interest to duplicate. His mother was the cog around which the family had prospered. With her gone too soon they felt rudderless and unanchored. His father a simple man was not familiar with the ways of the household. The lesson of uncertainty was never lost on her. They had wished for the children to study and create a niche for themselves. But, Maya had chucked all their plans within a nine month span.

Maya ? How come they came about to name their newborn such? Maya, not to be confused with mirage, the optical phenomenon the trick played by the light or the heat waves. Maya - meaning illusion, where things appeared as real but they were not what they seemed. Maya, did they just name the girl or did they understand the implication or was fate dealing them with some insulation some hint of times that would befall. Maya, the ephemeral. Maya, the ephemerae. Maya of no lasting influence. Maya the unprofessed one.. Maya !!

Maya was born to her mother, after a gap of five years. Munia and Munna, the youngest till then did not have a clue as to why all attention that was piled on to them until then was diverted to her mother initially and then to the new born. She disliked the little one. Money and Maya have similarities. They both have all running after them. They are both volatile in nature. Shifting moving fickle minded never stationary, unpredictable. Here today gone tomorrow. Some are bequeathed and bestowed to money while some have money thrust on them. While others labour for money and some utilise skills to make a kill.

Money presents itself to all alike. Suffice to say money comes Maya lingers. Some have hard earned money some hardly any money and some are hardly hit by the absence of money while some are hardly hit by money. It's the ones that abuse it who are hit hard by money. That is when Maya comes into play. One runs after it but Maya remains elusive. Like the proverbial carrot that is always within sight within reach, but always unattainable.

Mahadei her mother asked Munia to care for Maya. Munia felt restricted. In her ignorance she let the infant on the cold floor to tend for herself. She was unaware that wet nappies needed to be changed promptly. Elder sisters were known to look after younger siblings as a norm then.

Soon enough the baby fell seriously ill and the parents got alarmed. Pneumonia was the verdict pronounced by the doctor. That was when the Marwari neighbouring lady approached them again and told them of Munia's negligence, appending that she was too young a child to manage a child. Munia was not to be held culprit for the pneumonia, she stroked their ruffled feathers when they looked growlingly at Munia. They realised not all elder sisters had to have that aptitude and attitudes could vary. So, though she was directly involved in her sister's ill health, she was never made to feel so by her parents who took all the blame. Her father lamented at being unable to provide for the brood. Her mother was strictly asked to refrain from going out and take care of the newborn. Rest we shall see he brooded, what can be done how things can be managed. He was furious at his own inabilities.

It was over a year since her last misadventure. The Marwari lady ventured again assuming the time was ripe now to hit the red hot iron. She was the first to observe what Munia's parents bogged under the cover of responsibility did not, that the girl had potential. Her businessman husband left for his shop late in the morning after eating a heavy brunch, consisting of a full meal, to seal deals. Soon after he left she opened the presumably sealed window just a crack to bring in the sights and the sounds of the adjoining vicinity. This was her daily routine and escape from the lonely life in the big house. She marvelled at the commotion and the engrossed members of the family play out their parts in complete synchronisation day after day, she revelled in their drudgery too, not as a source of penury but as a source of living a full life of hardship and adversity.

Yet the parents fused qualities of togetherness of respecting women of speaking the truth of lies being punished on discovery of endeavour of laughter at the end of the day and of looking ahead to a new day. She soaked in their tribulations with awe and came to look up to the family with respect since she first stepped across the threshold of her house as a new bride. As the days passed by, slowly emboldened she would open the window wider and wider. Soon she was sometimes chipping-in in their chatter. Next she was in a Boolean relationship with them. Initially it followed the rule - A intersects B that is to say she was the common factor between the two families, her own and her neighbours to a little extent.

She was a businesswoman by birth and genes. She succeeded in her second attempt. She had judged that it would take at least three or four attempts before the proud mother gave in to her pleas. But the unfortunate incident of an ill Maya had worked in her favour and tilted the scales. So the now taller Munia who despised her conditions and younger sibling and was a school dropout and was becoming exceedingly unruly for the mother drenched in home work was without much reluctance allowed the permit, albeit with a heavy heart and great sorrow. Conceding young Munia to her fate, they tried to placate their doing. The condition she envisaged, A union B, that is to say everything common in both the families. Though she was an occasional visitor to their family Munia became a regular to her home.

She the daughter of one businessman married to another was delighted. She had a commercial outlook towards life. If she had any long term plans they remained latent. It was here Munia's mind trained for good thoughts and deeds diluted itself to suit purpose. Consistency in attitude was replaced by the conniving culprit cleverness. The intelligent path ahead compromised for the instant indulgence of now. In some circumstances, listen and comply told her mind, whereas listen and ignore told her heart. Sometimes the stand taken by her heart and mind interchanged their attitude, to her disgust. What is this she would wonder, cannot the two be in accordance why change and stand on conflicting sides? Torn between two seemingly opposite forces she devised her own path for endure and exist. If it benefitted her she complied if not then she propelled the ideas towards its cancellation, making excuses. Consequences were overlooked and the faltering heart or mind told to shut-up and remain in quietude without arising complications in the matter.

At some point her grandfather Ram Narayan was running a household of multitude of members, consisting of his sons and their families. On special occasions this number rose to 60, when his married daughters and their families gathered on visit. Ram Narayan was employed as driver at the government school across Navrang Talkies. He was a wise man and decided if his property was to be distributed it should be done in his lifetime. As far as he was concerned this would give his sons a good start. What happened later after he was gone was of no concern to him. Listen intently to my mantra for a pleasant life he told them. Earn Eat Enjoy together.

He had constructed a *timanjila* a three story house with a courtyard and a kitchen on the far end. The washrooms were towards the other periphery. So in a way though the household appeared to be together they were separate entities too. They were joint as well as detached. He allotted the lower portion to his eldest son Ramu, Munia's father. He gave one floor each to the other two younger sons. They were all married by now. All houses were made of brick, since the budget exceeded and became of constrain it was decided that the plastering would be done at a later date. The walls remained bare as they were while on construct

29

and never got the cement plaster pasted on them. In turn they never got the desired coat of white-wash during Diwali or on occasions of marriages in the family.

When his relations daughters and friends warned him candidly of his decision of wanting to see his sons settled in their own homes and its repercussions, he had heeded to their apprehension. He kept a room aside for his wife's picture and himself. The picture was a better replica of his wife by a budding artist in the neighbourhood, done in charcoal. Only his closest friend knew that he did not trust any of his sons to be bright enough to settle the matter amicably. In actuality apart from his friend only his late wife knew the real reason behind his eagerness. For he spoke to her often in soft hushed tones and whispers as if she were there next to him. He talked to her when alone and away from the milling grandchildren.

His wife was a strong willed woman who had run a big flourishing household. She was a strict woman who had got her daughters married at an early age and to the first family that came along wishing to marry their sons to her daughters. Marriages were made in heaven, *Ram milayi Jodi toh* she would curb any other opinion. The eldest was married to the son of a Sari shop owner in Hatia. All was fine with her she lived in a high rise house. She was also strict with her son's like her mother. When her school educated daughter in law's / *bahu's* arrived she could sense her position weakening in the hierarchy of things.

Things reached a limit the day her younger sister came visiting and instigated that she take charge of her educated wayward elder *bahu* who could be seen talking to all and sundry standing all day at the doorway. You keep sitting here all day and don't monitor your *bahu* who is becoming the talk of the neighbourhood. She may have attended school but does that give her a certificate to chitchat with all she claimed. Enraged thus she admonished her *bahu* upfront, a mother of two grown up children now. What is this you do all day, standing and talking to all who wander by? The lady did not budge. Infuriated enough now she bellowed her hand raised come inside or I'll give you one (slap).

Her timing could not have been more wrong. Being married to a businessman is difficult and being married to a Sari shop owner more so. For after showcasing sari's to customers for most part of the day he did not have the capacity, or the inclination to undo another she was heard saying to close friends in merriment. Women tend to take offence of their frustrations but when no one heeds they make light of it. It's their way of coping with the situation with dignity. If you cannot win it join it says the adage.

All her pent up dissatisfaction came to the fore. If she had crossed the limit in her mother in law's eyes the elder lady had over-crossed her limits too. The *bahu* retaliated, what wrong is it to talk. I am no newly married woman who needs to sit coyly with her head down. Times have changed but no you shall never change. What harm does talking bring in your evil eyes? You only talk of giving, here take this, as I indeed give you one she contemplated, the raised hand met the old lady's cheek even as she was completing her sentence.

Which of the two ladies was more astounded by the blow shall never be known. In the heat of the moment she did what she did, she told her husband, ashamed of her action and in complete guilt. On the spur of the moment she acted she told the policemen, who did not know the rules in reverse order. It was common practice to receive complains that a daughter in law was beaten up, but this was the first case to be registered where the protest went against the grain. The sister who had annoyed and aggravated the situation was questioned. The matter was finally rested by issuing warnings to both parties. The *bahu* sighed with relief so did the policemen at their incapability.

Womankind thrives on subjugation. That is not an entirely true statement. For the declaration needs clarification. For the singular word 'some' needs to be appended to it to make it a generalised statement. Some womankind thrive on subjugation. Most women are kind women too and others are kindly. Anyway, the elder lady was so stricken by the act and its repercussion that she never recovered from it and one day soon when she could not bear it any longer she put the whole matter to rest by pouring kerosene oil over her head and lighting a matchstick. As her mother in law wished as her last wish and warning, *the bahu* never did stood at the doorway again and was reduced to speaking in monosyllable.

Territorial? This one word is at the base of all vices. Continents Countries Premiers Governments Armies Navies Air Force's Policemen and Animals included, all fall under this category. It's a known fact. Wars are raged, battles are fought. Partition is called for; men fall and fail to adhere to standards they swore by. They blacken their hands and face in the colliery if push comes to a shove. But the unknown factor needs to be brought to light and acknowledged too. Women can be territorial too, within the confines of that hutment or apartment or thatchment or hatchment.

Munia entered into the Marwari wonderland, wide-eyed. A truly wonderful world opened up to her when she entered Jia's home. She adapted and adjusted to the change with ease. The immaculate and preen household appealed to her sensibilities. It was neat as a new pin yet it was crowded by things, in direct contrast to her sparse living packed with people. She was now a regular visitor to the Marwari family. She realised that furniture was also a part of decorating. They just possessed few chairs in her home and cots to sleep on. Their cloths were hung on a clothesline that ran parallel to the wall behind the door. She felt ashamed of the bare necessities whenever Jia visited her home. It always made her feel like she was dragging her short dress down to cover up some shortfall.

For the very first time she realised that homes comprise of items of luxury too. The Tv set attracted her most to the family. Tv opened up another new world for me. I could relate to the scenes being enacted, to the beauty they projected to the vistas they opened up to the dreams they showcased. I began to see my dreams being realised, *apne sapne poore karne lage* by watching movies and serials. I did not know her name then she said, but the leading lady of one particular movie her acting her chic manner of keeping her long strands of hair, loose. Her *ada* her style of flicking her tresses back by tugging her neck sweepingly. Her coquetry enchanted her. When her mother beckoned she left grudgingly.

It was here that Jia taught her and groomed her in household chores. But however hard she tried the girl remained adamant and refused to study her lessons, despite her potential. It was a two way bargain, wherein both the parties gained. She got to discover and be trained into the ways of the wealthy, while Jia got house help and company for herself. That was the time when I realised life was much more than eating playing sleeping.

Most afternoons Jia would take out her sewing kit and do some darning and mending of cloths as young Munia loitered on the indoor swing or jumped on the sofa with delight. She was awestruck at how patiently Jia sewed her torn and tattered garments and transformed them to suit her. Jia would stitch colourful petticoats and in time when her curiosity got the better of her Munia was initiated into the craft and soon learned to sew the blind stitch, now she would diligently hem the bottom loose edge of the petticoat. When her sewing did not come up to Jia's requirement when the *turpai* stitch would turn out shoddy she would undo the needlework without as much as a flinch and ask her to redo it till she was satisfied of the end result. The stitches had to be small and of even size, concealed from anyone's gaze at a distance of a few feet. When pleased with her sewing she would gladly show her appreciation by giving her 4 or 5 rupees for toffee.

In due time, I was stitching sari-falls, the border that is stitched to the underside of the free perimeter end of the sari so that the pleats fall gracefully at the feet of the wearer. Initially, she would ask me to hem the fall of worn sari's where the stitches had fallen apart. In the beginning I would place an inverted *thali* the round steel tray with edges beneath so that there was no bagging and sagging between the sari and the fall when I stitched them together. Jia insisted that the colours of both, the fall and the sari should be perfectly coordinated with the lighter shade of the sari. For the brighter shade of the fall would be visibly noticeable rather than remain inconspicuous. Giving allowance to the minor shade difference due to different texture of both the materials was tolerated albeit with some visible cringe.

Soon I was pretty much in demand by the neighbourhood women to stitch sari-falls for them too. I loved the work. No running errands just sit by the window watch Tv and be engrossed in work that furnished money. No one was complaining any more not even her mother or her protective brothers. Who initially created some scene at her being away with strangers? Now they waited for her to return and tell them the ways of the rich, their lifestyles their way of cooking their recipes.

Slowly and assuredly Jia initiated her into cooking, by initially asking her to assist the resident cook. Help me in cooking she would urge some afternoons when the cook went home on leave. When you prepare the dough not an iota of *atta* - wheat flour should remain sticking on the sides of the dish she would admonish. When your fist is smeared with the dough, you shall not open the lids of jars bottles pans and spoil them with smeared fingers, was her sermon. When you chop vegetables you should rinse them diligently first, only then shall you proceed to chop them into identical dimensions. Chop the onions for this slice the onions for that and grate the onions for another dish. Onion is onion how does it matter Jia I would protest then. It is not for you to question why, she would calmly reply. One day you shall learn on your own.

She was a hard task master. Some days she would insist that I roll the *chappati* the Indian wheat flour bread while she herself took up the task of roasting them on the hot girdle. She would apprise me with the finer culinary details. She taught me to make rice flour laddoo's which she ate during her fast. When I prepared these at my in laws place my *sasural* so to say, they were immensely appreciated by one and all. I still remember each of her instructions flung at me, measure this in the pan, chop the vegetables, add the sugar now, at this point remove it from the stove. She has now re-tailored some of the recipes. She would observe each of my task keenly, there was never any room for error. Omitting any step was sacrilege.

Give us the recipe of some favourite dish I compel her. She thinks for a moment I'll tell something that is tasty and can be made in a jiffy.

Mix together little ghee and maida (flour) and keep it covered. After 10 minutes sieve it on a sheet of paper now it should resemble sooji (semolina). For one kilogram of this sooji look-alike add 250 grams of roasted sooji. Pour half kilogram ghee in the wok. Add the above flour mixture and roast on a slow flame till it turns pinkish. Turn it into a large plate. Add one kg bhura (brown) sugar. Mix well till consistent. Add Cardamom powder and chopped cashew nut. Also add 250 grams crumbled *danewala khoya* (dried evaporated milk solids) to it and combine with care. Roll out the perfect laddoos. This is the famous Thaggu ke laddoo of Kanpur recipe she informs me with some self-importance.

She was the toast of her family now. Her brothers were soon insisting she cook the tasty food she was describing for them. She was reluctant in the beginning but readily agreed when they assigned some paisa for each task. Money, she understood this language well, the language she learnt while everyone presumed she was studying at school. Fortunate girl beamed her brothers on hearing her escapades of Tv viewing and those of having scrumptious meals at the

Marwari family. Fortunate, the word made her feel grand and blissful; she preened like a peacock and gloated at her glory. She seemed to convey – did I not say so, on my terms.

When Jia asked her for the meaning of her name she stood hapless. A little girl she explained. Is that so, questioned Munia? Then there is need for change, enough of this Munia Munia business. There is need for amend and need to be assertive and need to take charge of one's own life. So the first step towards it was to say goodbye to the diminutive Munia. And truly as perceived a new personality emerged with Aarti.

As the years slowly rolled by she had learnt all that was to be learnt from Jia. She had proved to be the best trooper any general could ask for. Jia's attention too got diverted by the fact that her brothers in law's children were adopted by her and her businessman husband, when her brother in law and his wife met with a fatal accident. Leaving the young children orphaned. Aarti could now be found in the kitchen galley doling out dishes she thought would appeal to the two new kids who had lost their parents so early on in life.

Soon she was assisting the rich Marwari neighbours in preparing tasty snacks and confectionaries for them. Next she could be seen going house to house independently making sweetmeats and savouries for the families to be consumed over the week along with their breakfast and evening tea. Gradually she would graduate to be an assistant cook and helping hand during marriages and ceremonies. Finally she was taking booking-orders for marriages, initially in Kanpur and later out of town too where her patrons took her with them. She was now assisted by two able assistants, who went along with her.

The Thakur's were to be her first employer. Three years we were with them. He gave employment to my husband and even taught him to drive as well as taught my children. On the day my husband whom I now call Bengali was to appear for his driving test so he could be recruited in govt service, he just could not raise his hand he was paralysed with fear I think. So he was employed as security guard. When the Thakur retired he called her husband and told him, your wife is more *kaamyab* successful and wise. Lead your life according to her judgment and opinion and you will lead a good life. Educate your children well also never lose hope he had finished.

He may have been a big officer but he had a bad reputation. We were in search of a house and none was available. He was tyrannical informed the ladies who worked for them earlier. His wife was obese and lay in bed mostly. I disputed that if I am upright then the others shall treat me right. And if I am correct then how someone can fault me and charge me as tainted. So armed with my appropriateness and in dire need of a roof over our heads I agreed to work for them.

Group activity and earnings which was our prime source of income had dwindled to nought, when my sister and brother in laws were married. We were slowly trudging back like a graph was retracing its parameters backwards. The up rise turned into a downfall. My children and my aspirations for them became of concern. Coupled with everyday nuisance in the home front and joblessness I decided to move on.

By then my parental home the three storey house at Phoolbag near Khedapati temple was sold. My brothers followed in my father's footsteps of taking loan that was to be their downslide. Meena my sister in law and I would go to the pharmaceutical firm for earning. She could read so she pasted the labels on to the bottles and I filled them up and checked them against the light for any impurity that may have crept in, she earned two hundred more than me. She was married off with these earnings.

I got to know of Cantonment area. When I visited it, it was *Jannat*, heavenly. Somehow I took a reluctant Bengali he found the pristine alluring. Then I decided that for leaving his parental home some *tamasha* would be needed, effervescence time. After two days of farce fighting's Budhaa retaliated. I got the perfect opportunity to leave home.

Some wisecracks from her are documented for all: One must listen to the heart it guides one well. What can be said of the mind, today it wants this tomorrow that and the day after it says other and later another.

Eating, feasting good and living well is imported, she used this word often referring to important. Of course I could have checked her but that I did not wish to do it might just as well curtail her and put her on the back foot. I could have easily edited the error too, but that would not be true to the story. So for all purposes I have gone ahead with the genuine. When asked to keep a book she would say.. in the Raibareli meaning library.

Cover the wok while cooking and cook fast food she said once. Fast food I repeated a smile beginning to form on my face which I found hard to curtail but coerced least she see it, undeterred she continued the heavy and snugly fasten lid of the pressure in the cooker decreases the cooking time you see. When you go northward to the mountains the cooking fires have to be stroked continually to keep the flames ablaze. She was in fact suggesting that the time to cook was proportional to the heat energy. Also that when the air pressure was lower foods take longer to cook.

She necessitated that the moon banes and increases during a fixed period. She was of course referring to the sinusoidal wave or the smooth repetitive nature of the curve, of nature.

She could make the homemade water heater fashioned from nails and a steel plate. Where did you learn this? I had put up a small-bulb manufacturing factory for my good for nothing husband she elaborated one fine day, he did not work regularly and the business had failed. He had erred again and she was clearly incensed.

Kerosene needed air to burn said her practical mind when I asked her as to why the lantern did not burst into flames when it had fire on one end and kerosene at the other? Okay by air she meant oxygen for the puritan here.

To divert her from her gushing self I would impede her flow by throwing in the proverbial clincher. What is the swiftest thing I once asked her? *Turant daan Maha kalyan* she presented after some reflection. Implying immense and instant beneficiation was the result of immediate charity. Shree Satyanarayana katha offers the same in its first chapter by articulating that this *vrat* this fast in *kalyug* the modern times gives the boon (reward) very quickly.

Knowledge comes but wisdom lingers say the Anonymous and *agyaat's* of the world. She was born to wisdom and knowledge lingered in the shape of silhouette always by her. Aarti why did you not go to school amused her employers? Academics had not lured her but the theories of the subject were not unknown to her. They had seeped into her knowing in a deflected manner. For she knew, that money was proportional to work. She also knew that work was inversely proportional to sleep. At one point in her mid age she was sleeping 4 hours a day. On approaching her doctor all her tests and reports came out fine, then the kindly lady enquired her of her day to day affairs. Not one to let such a brilliant opportunity of speaking of oneself she had regaled. You need to rest more Aarti admonished the doc. She took this singular piece of advice seriously. She knew and delighted in a strong body and illness never could pin her down for long. But age was catching up fast reckoned some to her. No she said firmly not wanting to pin the reason of her health wrongly on aging. It was her wayward husband she surmised clearly much to the chagrin of her family.

She wished for her husband to be a true foil to herself. Jia wished for her to marry a boy in their community who was slightly hand-handicapped. My parents thought about our community about our society. They refused. Jia insisted with me you are an adolescent just give your consent and I shall manage everything. But I was an obedient child. Not unless my parents agree she said. Her first suitor was dark. She declined. The second hailed from a well to do family. I told him I want to have a good life of eating out of going out. He said that was not the way they could conduct their lives in his home. All members were to be considered. She declined. She put up the same demand with Bengali. He agreed to her wishes, he saw to it that he could fulfil them too.

He came wearing bell-bottoms and appeared smart. Above all he was fair; a hundred shades fairer than her. In a society where a fair bride was the norm Aarti was seeking a fair alliance for herself. Fairness was a fetish fairness was guarantee for a good alliance fairness was the first stepping stone when a girl was considered by a family, fair child's parent rested assured of getting a suitable boy. These statements were all correct and could be said in all fairness.

When her mother in law came to see her she was not overtly impressed by her. But it was her mother in law's mother in law who openly and obviously appreciated the girl. She had her own reasons and thinking attached to it. She could see that young Aarti was a perfect answer to her own overbearing daughter in law. The elder lady had found a match in her who could stand up to the authoritarian girl she had conducted into her family many years ago, by just giving in to her fairness and beauty. Norms needed to be bended knew the old woman; it was high time rules were given a back seat and show the door. It was time to beat the trumpet loud and clear. It was time for triumph after decades of trials.

So she sent word and went up to meet Aarti in her room and pleaded with her *beta* kindly do agree to my grandson in union. You are skilled strong willed and talented and can take a stance if need be. Listen to this old ladies petition before considering answering. She who had seen many decades in her life knew and recognised spunk when she faced some.

Dear Aarti's constitution was built to confront anything mildly erroneous. Put her up against a challenge or anything unjust and she would literally bring her sari *aanchal* in a tight grip at her waist. All ready for a duel. She sent her consent. Her assent was considered a blessing by the old woman from her precious god's. She had prayed long and hard with utmost devotion so that god would relent and somehow send her some illumination that would end her misery, before her final exit. It was a bright moment in the greying woman's life, a moment to celebrate a moment to rejoice. Many grew wary of her overt contentment none could fathom the underlying reason underneath. In a swift turn of fates she had finally won.

In all fairness to her she had remained on the battle field for long. She endured dismal defeat after defeat, eschewing rout after rout knowing that all the hands were not dealt yet. She knew that a fair deal would be dealt sooner than later. God's are known to judge ones patience but its outcome is sweeter that nectar. Such yarns abound in mythology myth folklore and she had abundant belief in them.

Essentially she was happy that she was finally to get even with her ordering daughter in law. Of being granted to witness the day in her lifetime. Of knowing that she had a fair daughter in law but in turn her daughter in law would have a dim skinned one in return; this was no mean feat in her mind. Of being the more distinguished one finally. Of fair play.

If a Hindi movie song were to recapture the moment in song it would definitely be... *darbar mein ooparwale ke andher nahi parr deri hai, andher nahi parr deri hai.* If a dialogue were to represent the event it would be *mere karan arjun aayenge.*

She was selected by Bengali. Bengali is the name Aarti used, to refer to her husband, given to him by one of her employers.

On the day I stepped inside the threshold of my new home there was a gala party thrown and so there was a lot of commotion. It was the first wedding in the family of the new generation waiting in the wings to take wings and thus needed to be showcased as such. But when her parents did not pay the said amount promised to them strong undercurrents of dissent were clearly palpable to her. She was secure in the fact that her marriage was conducted as per everyone's wishes she could not gauge the soft whispers and raised eyebrows. She considered it to be some internal matter. That this party was to be indirectly funded by that alimony she failed to understand, for no such monetary promise was put forth to her parents or agreed by them.

The next day my brother came to take us, the newly married couple home as per tradition to conduct the *pag-phera* ritual, when the bride is supposed to go back to her parent's home for a day or two. This tradition seems a viable option when marriages were conducted within nearby environs or when the child was a child-bride. Anyhow, after dinner when Bengali was leaving he gave a folded beetle nut leaf to be given to me through my younger sister. I found his act very bold and wondered why he had done so. I do not eat *paan* and so my sister took it from me when I denied eating it. When she unloosened the conically wrapped leaf to see the contents inside she was surprised to see a small note hidden. She showed it to me but as you very well know by now I cannot read or write. I insisted with my sister to read the message written for me. It says I shall be back soon and I cannot live without you, she read aloud and went about the house teasing me.

The next day he visited Khedapati temple which was near my home, on purpose. My nephews and nieces would go there to attend the evening *Aarti* the evening prayers and to take the *Prasad* distributed thereafter. He cajoled them to go and tell your aunt that uncle is waiting for her. So I was literally dragged by the children to the temple. Wonder if he had bribed them with chocolates. So we sat in the temple premises and talked for long hours.

Soon it was time for me to go back to my husband's home. Once I reached there more rituals awaited, *Kuan pooja, nal pooja and ghat pooja*. That is worshipping of the well the tap and the river wharf. At each of these places I unknotted the bond secured by the ladies and the pundit at the commencement of the marriage ceremony. That evening, the children were sent across to give me company. Bengali would enter the room on some pretext or the other then go back then enter again then go back. When his *chukkar's* did not cease and after one round too many his mother annoyingly reprimanded him, *kahe ek jagah baithta kyun nahi hai re*, why don't you sit putt in one place son. To the younger children she admonished go to sleep in your new sister in laws room.

When Jia got to know that her marriage was fixed, she called her to come and be seated close to her. Then she gave her the most prophetic sagely advise. Do not answer back, respect your elders and try to appreciate your new family first. No sooner she stepped into her new home the foremost advice would come to occupy a major role immediately. For her mother in law Budhaa (the name suggesting an elder person) as Aarti now calls her, decided that the children of the house sleep with the new bride upstairs in the room specially constructed for the marrying son. While the groom slept with the male members of the family.

On the fifteenth day after her marriage she was to visit her parents again. That is when Budhaa took her aside and whispered, ask your father to give the amount he proposed to during the *'dwarchaar'* ceremony. When she drew a blank Budhaa asked her husband that he elaborate to her that as per the mediator of the marriage her father had promised some sum which he conveniently forgot and forgo-ed. On her return her sister in laws teased her as to how she found her husband to be? I don't know him; have not even spoken to him yet she stated simply. But staying away from your paramour is not correct did you not question, I thought custom required so, she answered in earnest. Jia's words had remained with her and she was wisely complying with them.

Alarmed by her uttering they spoke to their respective husbands saying something was amiss. The husbands in turn conversed with their father, who beckoned Aarti and calmly asked her, had her in laws said something to her. That was when she remembered the message to be delivered to her father. Her father sat aghast, appalled at the boldness of the mediator who had intentionally lied to both the parties. On one hand he had committed a huge amount on his behalf and on the other deliberately shied away from sharing this obligation.

The next day her husband stood at the doorway and was cheerily greeted by all the members of her family. Her father and brothers escorted him to the inner room. Then after enquiring about the well being of his family her father simply told him the facts. He also stated in a matter-of-fact manner that he would not send his daughter along with him, now. There was no way he could take the exceptionally huge burden of another loan in addition to the existing one.

Her brother's wife teased him we have not given you our daughter to toil if she does not get marital happiness she better be here. He thought they were teasing him and so he laughed along at the banter hidden behind the truth.

Though his mother had sent him with instructions to bring back his wife only when the amount promised was furnished, he acted like an honourable man with a just mind of his own. He assured his newly acquired father that all shall be fine and he had come to take his bride home. A relieved household rejoiced at god's mercy, for solving the matter amicably and for finding them an excellent son in law. After much fanfare eating and singing she headed back with him.

Back home he took charge of the situation and declared that the sleeping children be brought downstairs. The sleepy household did not create much of a commotion and hurriedly herded the kids to their grandparents and parents cots. Infuriated and highly incensed raged his mother silently, she was not going to take this insult lying down. She felt the son whom she held so close to her bosom was being snatched away. The detachment was unbearable. Each pore of her body flamed and she felt hot and ablaze with fury. Her wrath consumed her peace of mind.

Alone with his wife now he felt like the marathon runner who had lost fifteen vital seconds after the pistol round had been shot, indicating 'go'. His mind was consumed by the beauty of his sleepy wife. He felt each pore of his body ablaze with passion. The fifteen days of detachment was now getting to be unbearable. He held her tightly such that no one could snatch her away. Soon they were lying down.

Despite his failings he rose in her eyes. For there are some who remain tethered to their imaginary umbilical cord? No harm in clinging such, if it be for the right and just cause of showing gratitude to one's parent and elder. For when a conniving lady demands of her son that he beat his wife, a man needs to ascertain and reassess his priorities.

Insecurity leads a woman to go against another and a man to go against another. It's not gender specific; it's a known fact of living in this world, sea or jungle. So we can safely say it's a trait displayed by all living mannerism, mammals and non mammals included, vertebrate and non vertebrates incorporated. An actuality, that prevails over mankind, like the gloomy fog most mornings. It's there for sure, but it's invisible too. It's a common occurrence but vanishes into nothingness within no time. Perceive it one can, but point it touch it none. It remains dimensionless unit less and clueless.

The difference between fog and mist is a very visible factor called visibility. Generally, it's called fog when the visibility is one kilometre or say one thousand and one hundred yards or lesser. Else it is known as mist. One can thus safely presume that mist is the bigger umbrella and fog its smaller version, as the spelling suggests too. Wonder why it remains unit less in such a scientifically advanced earth. Wonder too if they would name the unit after me, after all... you know what I mean.

Btw since we are on the topic, did you know that mist appears bluish and haze brownish in pictures. Mist is elegantly depicted by A J Cronin as 'a pure white mist crept over the water like breath upon a mirror.' Security provides for a secure environment and insecurity is known to unfasten the secure.

From the very beginning to the very end he held his father in law in great respect. Many an evening's they sat on the chairs in the verandah and chatted on various matters. When money grew short his mother in law would simply claim Babu we can just offer you what we eat, some bread and a little curry. He ate what was served without a fuss. He always came back and spoke highly of her family. She would remain indebted for all his sensitivity and sensibility shown towards her family.

He loved visiting her home and the bonhomie atmosphere. The men mostly tended to the male relatives and guests. Later her mother began conversing with him as she would with her sons. But this was not the norm, credit must be given to her husband for he chose to be treated like a son and not as the son in law, she believed. So later, when they would take leave after spending a couple of days at her place, her villager mother would reprimand him. Rajinder babu she would say look after my girl with utmost care or I shall pull your ears I tell you. He would take her admonish in the right spirit and tell her he would always abide by her.

Her mother always harboured the uneasy fact that some day if his mother wished so, he would leave her daughter alone again. When she was born her mother had visited the family pundit to cast the infant's horoscope. After he read the charts in deep concentration with some consternation he had told her mother that the constellations are foretelling her child would face sorrow after her marriage. How long shall this period be she had enquired with worry lines beginning to form on her forehead? Some quick calculations later he had said 30 years. Wonder if he was referring to the *dasha* (period) of Jupiter followed by the *dasha* of Saturn that would be afflicted. On sighting her crestfallen face he had brushed aside the first statement by gushing in another. After that she shall meet someone in tandem with whom she would rise and grow above the rest.

She looked up at me in delight and apprehension. Who me? Yes you. Don't you put me on any pedestal I warn her. I think you shall meet 'yourself' after 30 years I lead her on to the right path. That's correct you are so much like me. I mean the 'you' in 'you', I say for clarification sake or maybe 'your god, I deflect the unwanted attention. She is not amused.

Interval

Soon she was eager to furnish much and at great speed her thoughts wandered from incident to incident. When the gush turned to babble it was time to contain her. Listen Aarti have you seen the movie Sholay? Is there anyone who hasn't she looked up from her work eyeing quizzically, its aired on Tv also so often. I let her extra remark go unnoticed. You remember that dialogue, Basanti as long as your feet dance Veeru's breathing shall persist. In a similar fashion I wish to inform you that as long as you have something to say this story will be penned. *Jab tak tumhare pass kuch kehne ko hoga tab tak yeh kahani chalegi.* She was damn pleased. She understood that there was breathing space and she could curb her pace.

Soon I was to learn that she was prone to minor accidents too. Every now and then she would come to say she had skidded or slipped or had a fall. Soon she knew that I would retort and tease her 'you are a very fallen woman Aarti' when she reported a fall. It was a joke we shared and laughed loud at.

One day she asked me to give my contact number to her in writing. Amused I asked her how you were managing all this while. My daughters would dial the numbers for me she blurted. Okay fine, just as I was about to write she barged with a request, in Hindi. So began a lot of deciphering. Firstly I decoded the 10 digits from English to Hindi and put them on paper for her. She in turn would decode them again to punch the appropriate numbers on the phone tabs. But do you know where the corresponding numbers are. Yes she readily nodded pleased. Where is *nau* #9 I test her, she promptly indicated to the right marking? Did I say somewhere she was unlettered?

Suppose you were to meet Rekha ji someday? She does not believe me an iota, there is no semblance of joy reflecting in her eyes. She sees I'm a little crestfallen so she says if I can talk to Rekha on the phone that would be more than sufficient. She does not believe, but I do.

Second Half

People follow ordinary lives. People follow extraordinary lives too. This was true of people belonging to all strata of the so called society as well as the hinterland as well as the hunter-lands. Slog slaughter sleep was the established ordain of the ordinary. But in instances where these adjectives were replaced and repainted by sheen strive strength they resemble the extraordinaire. The action is called Patina. Pain endured leading to gain. It's the appearance of an aura around someone that is attained from association, habit, or established character.

Fear have you known it at any point in your life, the feeling of fright, of the world crippling and crumbling around? I'll not tell lies she supplemented. Yes I have felt fear and frustration. She epitomises Gurudev Rabindranath Tagore's poem to the hilt. Where the mind is without fear and the head is held high.

The complete poem goes thus.

Where The Mind Is Without Fear

Where the mind is without fear and the head is held high
Where knowledge is free
Where the world has not been broken up into fragments
By narrow domestic walls
Where words come out from the depth of truth
Where tireless striving stretches its arms towards perfection

Where the clear stream of reason has not lost its way
Into the dreary desert sand of dead habit
Where the mind is led forward by thee
Into ever-widening thought and action
Into that heaven of freedom, my Father, let my country awake.

True it was written for the awakening of India, but it could well impersonate an individual.

Life would be a dream after marriage she dreamed. If it was not she would make it one, she had resolved to herself. Life must be led the way it was supposed to be led, with dignity. No cutting corners here, no compromise, no doing up with that stale bread or roti with pickle for her. She wished to live full and wanted a full plate served in front of her, to the delight of some and to the soreness of others.

Her mother knew that Budhaa was a powerful lady and wielded an iron fist in her home. Though she was not to be blamed directly for the fifteen day fiasco, for it was the middleman, who had brought the families together was to be blamed. But her behaviour after the marriage remained appalling. How nice it would be if she would have taken an appealing stance.

When we received the proposal from Bengali's family we were told that he worked in the cloth mill. Preliminary investigations by my family suggested that he was a good guy. The marriage was conducted as per tradition. Few days into the marriage and Bengali stopped going for work, he stayed back at home. He worked at the mill, this statement was partly true. He worked there on a temporary basis; this part of the aforesaid statement remained unstated. And so soon after marriage he was laid down from work for six months. When I started pestering him about work his mother suggested he join the paper mill at a reduced salary.

For the next day onwards her insinuations began. On one pretext or another she would implicate Aarti as soon as her son came home from work in the evening. Take charge of her she would holler, he would come charging at her bang the door close. Then proceed to hit the door all the while shouting at her. Later he asked her to make some noise when he mock tormented her for the sanctity of the house. But Aarti was not made of some immature amateurish elements. She was a thorough bred who knew how to stand up for their rights. She refused to entertain and be part of any slipshod and sloppy antics.

Why she questioned should I go along with false pretences, just to please your mother. What of my mother? When the neighbours shall carry the tales across to her what is she going to presume? That like her elder daughters she had a torturing husband too, which is as far away as can be from the truth. When her sister Parvati married, every now and then she would be back to her parents. In tatters underfed and bruised. When a young Aarti saw this, she asked her sister if her husband had done this to her. Why do you stay quiet, why don't you give it back to him in the same manner. Appalled at her younger sister's concern and conceit she would laugh at her. God forbid if you get such a husband, wonder what you shall do. Why wonder I'll tell you right away I'll give him back in the same coin.

Those who worked for the Lal-imli cloth mill lived in the vicinity called Lal colony, the red colony. Nearby was the Safed colony, the white colony where paper mill workers resided. One uncle would come from Safed colony to visit our home every day. Budhaa would ask me to make and serve assorted dishes for him; initially I wondered that he must be some revered elder of the family. But soon doubts cropped in, when my mind began to wander. Why did he come when the men of the house were away? Why not when they were home?

So I switched tracks and became friendly with the children. Then innocently I asked them who this uncle was who comes to meet Budhaa often. Everyone called my mother in law Amma but because of her behaviour I never could bring myself to utter her name. Initially I almost did without calling her by her name, by just stating what needed to be said, without any preamble or nomenclature.

When they said that he was not related to them, I understood something was drastically wrong. On enquiring my neighbour hinted with a chuckle that maybe he was her childhood paramour. Whereas my Budhaa is tall beautiful and fair he was dark and dismal looking. That evening I straightaway asked my father in law Babu why does this uncle come here? Why do we have to cook for him when there wasn't sufficient for the family? He told me the whole story. I told him you step aside and let me handle this my way.

When uncle appeared on the doorstep the next day I refused to cook for him. Budhaa was greatly annoyed. She howled he is our friend and guest how can you refuse him foodstuff. If he is our family friend tell him to come by in the evening. This is a house of growing girls and daughter in laws now. There is no need to visit us when the men are not around I informed him. I was about to hold his collar but before that he slipped out without a word.

My life was hunky dory. We started going out together. We visited the Phoolbag area we saw films in Naurang Talkies where the first class fare was two rupees fifty paisa. I hear the cost now has risen up to rupees three or four hundred. We would eat *chaat* at the park and we would talk a lot. I would tell him the ways of the rich and how he needed to learn some refined manners. He was a willing partner, not like most of my friend's husbands who treat them like dirt, while they are the dirty ones.

Budhaa did not like any of it. She became hostile and would ask me to get up at 3 o'clock in the morning. For lunch boxes needed to be ready by 5am, when the men left for the mills by bicycle. I would cook sweep swab scrub wash cloths without uttering a word. If Bengali interfered she would shut him up by saying don't become your wife's slave. She is my daughter in law and I need to teach her the ways of the house.

Those days' condiments like turmeric coriander red-chilly cumin would be freshly grounded every day. The palm of my hands would hurt with so much workload. She insisted that I finish off all cooking chores in a spate. Reasoning rightly that more coal would be required if one worked slowly. She was judiciously consuming the resources and thereby stretching her expenses further. But those days I failed to appreciate her logic.

By afternoon sleep would engulf me. She refused my urge saying that no one sleeps in the day time in our house. This is the time to clean the wheat, rice and pulse grains to chop vegetables to.. to gossip with the neighbourhood I would complete her sentence. Six months went by thus. Happily I had adjusted to the daily responsibilities entrusted to me.

But my health began to show tell tale signs. There was no system of breakfast here only two meals a day was the norm, lunch in the morning and dinner at night. Slowly and carefully I started grooming the young children and moulding the house as per my desire.

Most afternoons the ladies of Lal colony could be seen perched under the huge Neem tree in the playground the huge *maidaan* at the centre. That is when our neighbour across the wall called for me. She passed over two bricks which she said I should use to step on. I placed one brick over the other and stood stretched over it. I was eye to eye with my neighbour a village woman. Without any preamble she uttered, every day I listen that you are listening to all that Ramawati aunt is asking you to do. The more you bend the more you shall be allowed to bow and be bogged down. That is a rule of life.

One always considers and is of the view what can a rural woman know? Like this neighbour of ours or my mother. But some of the most sagaciously wise advice I have received from them. In fact the crusading attitude I display is an attribute I absorbed from this woman right ahead of me, advising me to not relent but retaliate.

You see I was keen to marry. Even as a child I would frolic about and tell my grandfather, when I grow up I shall marry, then I shall do this fashion then I shall do that in my house. It's a very inherent element in girls that can be seen to be on display ever so subtly when they begin to play with dolls. When they want to know how babies come about? Not many boys' display these attributes not many ask about the origin of babies; they are more into playing outdoors with balls and marbles. No wonder then that Barbie dolls is a big industry. Grandfather would laugh out aloud and tell my mother take care of this daughter of yours, ever so ready to marry, does she even understand what marriage entails?

Like I was saying I was too infatuated to get married to put the scarlet red *sindoor* on my hair parting, to paste the big bindi on my forehead to wear the maroon and golden bangles to jingle them to wear new saris every evening and wait for my husband to return from work. She was enamoured and smitten by Rekha in the film Aalap. She wished to emulate her and her style in the film. Most probably the first film she saw on the Tv at Jia's.

Maroon and golden bangles I question her entertained? Which colour would that be can you just point them for me for reference and writing sake. She looked around and spot on she spotted the maroon on the tablecloth and the golden bangle. Her ways fascinated. What other colour do you know pink is there white is there black is there. She learnt of the colours when she worked for the Bengali family, where the lady wore colourful cotton saris and requested her to bring out the red or the green or the yellow sari from the cupboard for her.

Work, more work or less work was not of any concern to me. I complied with any that was told. Only when after one of her neem-tree gossip sessions did my Budhaa come and tell me not to comb hair in the evening did I speak back to her. Why what does combing hair damage? All my work is done and it does not entail a single paisa? It brings bad luck she countered. How does it bring bad luck, if I do not work that shall bring bad luck, I reasoned? She has an analytical brain give her reasons and she would listen to any counsel but show her the blind-faith and she would scoff.

At the paper mill Bengali was soon to fall in bad company and became one like his father. Boozing away and creating some filthy scene or the other when home.

It was my first Diwali after marrying; Bengali learnt from his friends that they were gifting their wives some present or the other. What gift he enquired? Household items utensils or sari's they guided him. On his return that day he told Budhaa, Amma Babu shall be getting bonus so get one sari for Aarti this festival.

It was an innocuous request, a show of his appreciation for her. But the elder lady was incensed and infuriated on hearing him. Maybe she was having a bad hair day. How dare you, how dare you she repeated and questioned at the same time, how dare you put forth such a demand?

It was evening time and I was in the kitchen frying hot *poories*, the deep fried bread. When I heard of the commotion between son and mother I rushed out to smother it. I placated my husband why insist for a sari, have I asked you for one, let go your claim. But he was adamant and insistent that she buy a sari for me. Listen, he now admonished me you work round the clock do I interfere. No. Now she has to get you a sari he claimed undeterred. What shall your parents feel when you go home to greet them for the festival, that you have come to this house merely for working. Somewhere at the back of his mind was the quip made by my sisters in law.

Those were the days my husband really cared for me. No one could say a word to me or against me. He can still not hear a word if you go and tell him now that Aarti is awful he will stand up for me. He may not talk to you generally on seeing you but shall not listen to any lying down. He knows your worth I claim. Yes that is the matter, in most households she quips, men know the worth but that makes them insecure. They disown worth but at what cost? But worth is lotus-like; it flourishes surrounded by the marshes and stands tall. Worthless cannot a worthy stand.

When Budhaa heard his words infuriated and singed she went to the kitchen held the wok by its handles and came out shaking with wrath. Oh my god I wondered what was the lady up to on this festive season, the deep frying pan contained splutter hot oil. To everyone's relief she drained the smoking oil into the drain. Thus she felt gladdened after spoiling the festival, *teohar poora kharab kar dein.*

That was not to be the end of his mother's warring woes. Soon she demanded we separate from the family and look out for a house of our own, only then you shall understand she mocked. Why look for another house we shall stay here only as this is not your house. You did not get it from your parents. It's for all of us Bengali demanded. Somehow I mediated and pacified both.

My well wisher neighbour on the other hand met with a tragic end. She had a daughter and a son and was expecting her third child. One night we heard wails from her house. On seeing me leave for her house Budhaa prevent me saying you shall not leave this house. Why I questioned her no religion is greater than humanity. If she is in pain I shall go find why she wails thus. On seeing her condition I asked her mother in law why what happened? Oh it's nothing she complains because she does not wish to work. She was fine as long as her husband was with her, he went for his duty and this forsaken woman begins to yowl.

Look at her she needs care immediately. I could see her slip into an unconscious state. I called for my husband for help he come immediately. Budhaa too came after him and demanded he come back. So he left. I could not bear to see her deteriorating condition. I pleaded with the elder woman to take her to the hospital. Hospitals were in their nascent stage in those days. Where is the money she pleaded? Hiolett Hospital is free of charge we'll take her there. First let me get a rickshaw for her. When Bengali heard me he came forward to get the rickshaw.

We laid her in my lap and rushed on as her younger sisters in law Munni looked on frightened. Word got around. The child was born even without the doctor's assistance. Her husband had arrived by then he took the son and just comfortably forgot his wife. How can husbands not have love for their wife? She who bore all was critical and the doctors had warned that if she endures till 5 o'clock in the morning she shall survive. She clutched on to me and would not let go of me. Her son has grown tall now and touches my feet on meeting. Looking at him gives me great happiness. Munni became my friend. She assists me and looks after my bank accounts in Kanpur.

Anyway we did not separate nor left home. But every now and then the two got into some spate some dispute some argument. I was happy as long as she was not coming after me, so frankly speaking it hardly mattered much. It seemed they had signed an imperceptible agreement not to agree on anything agreeably. Three years went by thus, happily married.

When no child was born to us in three years matters took a serious turn. Initially I warded off claims for a child saying that we do not intend to have children so soon. But now my quip seemed faltered.

Now our intentions were open to discussion and dissection. Budhaa came up with her neem-tree logic saying that since she was tall and he short they could not bear children. Slowly the gravity of these harmless scoff increased their acceleration and reached a crescendo with scornfully naming her a barren women.

The word is a banned and barred article from every single woman's dictionary. Fertility of land and woman are considered auspicious. That year when the festival of Nauratri arrived I spread my *aanchal* the loose end of my sari with my hands in complete reverence and asked goddess Durga for a child to be given unto me. It appeared that I was spreading a basket for the child to be delivered into. I cried to my heart's content Ma I sobbed you do not know the harsh words I have to listen to to the barbs that sting the tongue that spews acerbic remarks, bless me devi Ma.

Relieved thus, that now my worries were in Ma's hands, I walked back home. That month with Ma's blessings I conceived, miraculously. I could not cook for the flavours that arose while cooking made me sick. I threw up often. But relentlessly I went on with my chores. I would tie a scarf over my mouth and nostrils, thereby cutting off the aroma rising from the dishes.

I was not gaining much weight; I was all stomach and no body so to say. When my brother came to visit and saw me in this condition he immediately cooked up a narrative, saying that our mother was not keeping well. So if Budhaa would allow Aarti to come home for a week. My brother was a wise man when I started answering back to my elders he was summoned. I sent word for him that he was not to interfere and there was nothing I could not manage on my own. When they questioned him on my behaviour, he stated in a manner of matter of fact that when we sent her after marriage she was not like this. What happened in the ensuing years that she replies back is for them to consider. I was so proud of him.

Back home I was pampered like a lost child who has been found. Sweetmeats fruits and snacks were specially prepared for me. When Bengali saw that that is how I have to be cared for he made a mental note to look after me thus. On my return he brought some *rasmalai* sweet that evening. Since money was scarce he did not get any for the whole family. I was so naive that by the time he was in the bath I went and placed one nibble in every members mouth, Budhaa included.

Oh what frenzy she created. Within moments the house brimming with joy turned into a crazy place. She pointed fingers at Bengali she accused him of favouring the wife of a few years. Of, forgetting the respect of parents and the learning's of elders of becoming a bonded slave to his wife. Just because he had come out from taking his shower he remained cool for some time listening with patience the accusations being flung like an automatic ak 47.

When he presumed that enough was enough he gestured at her to stop, to curtail her verbosity. To, conclude the non-issue then and there. Did not everyone get to taste a bit of the sweet? Whereas utterance of the right word at the right time can be the cause for magical moments expressing a wrong word can bring about a delusion deluge of hallucination.

Well by now the coolness had evaporated and the son a replica in some senses of his mother and the harbinger carrier of her genes erupted too. Tell me does not father get Jalebi's for you every now and then he spilled the beans. The whole household is aware of it but we choose to shut our eyes. It makes us feel good that he cares for you. Budhaa stood motionless it seemed someone had cut off the electricity to the projector and the scene on the screen remained frozen. In a huff she stomped to her haven her shelter from prying eyes and wagging tongues. She had forgotten the cardinal rule, when one points a finger at others three hidden one's point at themselves too. Pin drop silence prevailed where jarring voices were being raised.

After that day Bengali would give me money to buy stuff I wished to eat, he respected Budhaa's wish tactfully. But he was borrowing money from friend's relations neighbours ex employees. It was five months since he was laid down from job, again. The initial three months the employer of the mill rested him and the later two months he was laid down with acute lower back pain. By the third trimester passing of each day was a matter of huge concern.

It's not anyone's fault except our misfortune. How long could Budhaa continue to feed us especially since money was scarce, she also needed to marry off her two daughters. Since five months we had not contributed towards the joint-family purse. So with a heavy heart one sad day she called us and suggested that we separate our kitchens.

However good or bad times we may have been through but we both carry each other in much regard and mutual respect. Now Budhaa never tires from praising me to the sky and I reverently perform my duties towards her. Someone has very rightly claimed that people are not appalling only circumstances are.

I know how difficult a decision this must have been for her. But at times display of harsh attitude is the only solution to end an embargo. Anyway we began our independent life together. We went to my mother's and made her aware of the situation. Quietly she gave us some money. On our return we purchased some rice pulses and wheat flour.

Her son was born by then and one fine day she received an urgent message from Jia. That she should come and meet her at once as there had been a raid in her husband's newly opened jewellery shop. Immediately she scooted with her son in her arms to her parents. Here she left the infant in her mother's care stuffed some foodstuff in a tiffin box and headed across to Jia's.

Inconsolable Jia related that the police had raided the showroom premises early in the morning and had escorted Chachu to the Police station. When the two orphaned children arrived at the household about a decade ago, they began calling Jia's husband Chachu. Aarti also and now the entire neighbourhood was calling him Chachu, literally meaning the younger brother of their father. The new jewellery business was an expansion and extension of the existing sari business to accommodate and initiate the young man into the family dealings.

Aarti headed straight for the police station and sent word to her elder brother who by now had risen to a position of some eminence in the Janta Party, the ruling party at the time.

When she saw her Chachu sitting on a chair surrounded by junior staff on a hot and humid day she was grieved. She took charge of them. Do you know the *kanoon* the law she badgered? He is my Chachu most revered in the community he has just opened up a new shop and you feel he has done some wrong. Leave him let him go she hollered. Her brother rushed to the spot with some recommendations. I do not know what business transpired but Chachu was allowed to go a free man. By evening Chachu returned back home. When the house bell rang Jia was unsure who would be at the door, definitely not her husband. When Jia saw them both she let out a shrill voice of joy, elated. It appeared she was meeting her husband after a long sojourn. She held Aarti in her arms and would not let her go.

Bewildered Chachu just could not believe what had hit him. A day before he and the family were rejoicing and celebrating Diwali together. He had spent the entire day within the clutches of the law. But now was miraculously home by evening. More so he was shocked that little Munia whom he never as much as looked at with some potential was the factor who mobilised the machinery for his release and relief.

Unable to put into words his silent appreciation of her he gestured at his wife, she? His eyes looked at Jia questioningly, she, of all she? Yes our girl our Munia our Aarti the one who trained under me my trooper my pride. Fight injustice with the ferocity of a tigress did you teach her that asked the husband lovingly. Her head held high Jia nodded, but when he did not withdraw his adoring gaze she looked the other way coyly. Love being timeless does not perceive age as an obstacle, it percolates unmindfully.

Her three children were born by then. Her home did not come to resemble anywhere the home of her dreams. Each day was a burden, each living moment a misery. In that very state she felt fear grip her and she left her home hearth and children. Blinded with terror she wandered about then found herself in front of her childhood friend Beheniya's house. Who let her in and did what she could do best, listened to her tale of woes. Once the fury abetted she calmly tutored her to the facts of practicality. Remarry she suggested or try and reflect on your daughter's plight when left alone without your care. The word daughters brought her back on track. One day and one night she spent at Beheniya's. She did not give in to the abysmal no way, word was sent to Bengali assured he came and took her home.

On the day she returned from Kanpur, though she sounded drained, she let the dams of her insecurities flow in a verbal gush. I listened to her torrents, completely overtaken by her pouring of the events of the days gone, of the catchment drain so to say. When towards the end of her narrative, when she got repetitive in her stream I had the urge to get my notebook to jot down a few effects. She was speaking from her heart she said God had given her a good heart she needed to be thankful to Him. While others procrastinated she listened and did as her heart told. I let the urge pass. Later when I told her about the urge, saying I wasn't sure she could re-recount with as many emotion, passion and expressions, she said god does not let me forget my story. The moment I think there is respite from the doldrums he sends a new dilemma. All humdrum is spun out of the window in an instant.

That day when the telephone bell rang she was narrating about her infancy. Her mother called her, the one who had met god and come back to her. This incident was narrated so often, it lodged and locked into her young mind. When her father returned after a day of cycle repairs his loincloth was smeared by the black of the lubricant. She had tried different soaps scrubs styles to clean the garment, to her dismay each technique failed her. Erase of this grease was a nightmare for her mother, till she hit upon the idea of poison treating poison. She smeared the greased blotch with kerosene oil. The lodged splodge of dirt magically displaced with ease. She had reasoned reasonably.

Her husband a stickler was tickled at her wash-ability, appeased with the whiteness he asked her for a demonstration the next morning. She could barely wait for the next day to emerge at the eastern horizon. Feeling self-important she yanked the gathered unstitched cloth from the peg, where her husband had hung the dhoti the previous evening. Puffing her chest high she loosened the loose dirt by giving the gathered garment an unexpectedly swift but whooshing jerk. Her husband wondered and smiled inwardly at the effusively fulsome gesture of his dear wife. Outwardly he remained unruffled least she become conscious of his glance and glee. Focused like a magician in his Act, with elaborate gestures she dabbed the acquired blemish with kerosene oil or *mitti ka tel* as was regionally known.

The name must have originated from the fact that the oil was procured from earth, which in Hindi literally meant *mitti*. And with utter delight for her and the household gathered about her, Puff! she would elaborate to her daughters and sons tweaking her middle finger and thumb the soiled was restored to the new. The family circle dispersed stumped. Mornings was a busy time for all the members, who believed in utilising sunlight to the maximum benefit. This way they could spare and save a little more by not utilizing the kerosene filled lantern till late in the night. It was the way of the early man it was a natural way which was slowly giving way to the ill sought breed of late risers.

Before she proceeded to the corner of the open courtyard to wash the cloth she handed the glass bottle to her husband. Assuming he knew its rightful place up and above from the growing children's reach, on the top niche in the wall she called *aala*. He who had not ventured much in these parts of the quarters was unable to find the bottle-cap perched and hidden from view. A strict disciplinarian he rushed to his shop a little flustered at the demonstration and subsequent delay. Women he wondered are never capable of understanding timekeeping.

He, Ramu Shrivastava was married young to a younger Mahadei. She belonged to the village of Maharajpur. She was aged five and he was barely a few years elder. A year later it was decided to bring her to the home of her marriage, as his mother fell grievously ill. She proposed she could thus impart the ways of the household to her next generation and become free of any obligation of not having performed her duty fittingly. Mahadei arrived at her new home wearing a frock. She was pampered by the elder woman. The woman would cook *kabulichana* / chick pea on the fire for her and feed her using a sleek stick as fork when she was reminded of her parents and home and also when she refused to eat. How a lady conducted herself was paramount in a society gripped in the shackles of gender vice and gender vices. Here, the foremost vice significant of being a subordinate, the second vice specifying immoral behaviour.

She often narrated this to her children with gratitude with fond memories of her new life in the house of her husband of the woman who groomed her well for the vicissitudes. Munia learnt the lesson well from her mother. That, come what may, she had to tend and fend for her family on her husband's earnings or as she was to later learn on her own, by her own means.

Peril struck immediately. Ramu was summoned by the police. A case was registered against him. The superintendent has summoned you, you nasty man they roughed him up. A man of little means but a man of conviction he was not perturbed. What is the matter he questioned the two men in uniform. Shun the innocent act mister the two growled at his obstinate attitude. Ahh haa he thinks he can go scot free they interjected. What is the matter brother he prodded a little alarmed, now? Really you do not know, they wondered aloud at his cunning, you are going to be a hard nut to crack, they interpolated. Now his composed calm pose bewared at the unknown. What is it he pleaded what is it he repeated, do tell me what has befallen? Taking heed of the man tremble with the untoward they suggested it would be better to keep him in the dark. That you shall hear from our Sahib they postulated at the crestfallen.

He left the open bottle on the floor where it could be detected by the woman on her return. She, he could hear her descending on the steps leading to the terrace after she spread the garment on the clothesline. He was oblivious of the fact that the bottle with dull yellow contents lay precariously unattended; he was unaware of the toddler who had followed behind. Peril struck.

While most used brain like a daily wager she used hers like an entrepreneur, thinking logically ahead setting the trend, following the star using feedback to upgrade and reinvent.

Her mother taught her ward just two lessons. Not all were equally equipped to grasp her lessons of life to the same extent. Like the fingers of the palm each child inherited infused inculcated only that which it could assimilate from that which was being served. What appeared to one as chaff and chimera was to the other of worth and capital. She taught them that no matter what any of them would rob – rob one of money and matter or anyone of their *haq*, that which is entitled to someone. Secondly all work should be looked upon with dignity and decorum. Even if one were to fall on bad times never wile away time in wallow. This work is beyond me that this work is below me that this work is not bullish. Work is work respect it as worthy, respect it that it came your way revel in it rejoice in it: don't underrate it. Not others but only you can demerit your works worth, remember. She would saunter about her work as she sermon them, knowing full well that not all her brood was adept at learning and retaining her broach her approach to lay down the lines for the right of a right life.

Aarti's elder daughter Rinki fell seriously ill. We were residing at Cantt area by then. It was the day of the *Janamashtmai*, the birth celebrations of lord Krishna. She was very young then. I was busy with my work when my harried neighbour called me to hurry. On reaching home I saw that she was sitting her face and body covered in vermillion powder. She wore the red scarf the *chunar* over her head. I have no idea if she had consumed the powder but soon she fell unconscious. The Bengali family I was working for took us to various hospitals different and diverse tests were conducted she spent her time and money on us. Rinki would hallucinate; only my *mata rani* my devi Ma brought her back to us.

It so happened that a woman caught fire and expired. When I went to her house Rinki who never let go of me lingered and followed me unknown to me. After that she fell ill. She would not stop crying. We took her to each and every hospital we were guided to. Lastly we took her to the Muslim hospital they also could not treat her. Many relatives got upset on knowing about my taking her to this hospital. But I did not care; blood relation is above all religion.

Bengali would call on all the doctors' fall on their feet bang his head on their foot and cry for help. Save my child doctor save my child he would wail. That is why I say he is the best husband a wife can wish for. I always pray and bless that the daughters of my well wishers and known get a husband like mine.

While rushing from door to door from one hospital to another in frenzy I did not get even a moments respite. When the doctor said that now it's up to the god's only, I remembered I had forgot my god's. Abruptly I was reminded of my goddess Tapeshwari temple. Possessed I rushed to the temple bare feet without informing anyone. It was afternoon time when I reached the temple the doors to the temple were about to shut. I barged in and pleaded in front of the idol of *devi ma*. The priest heard me and offered me *sindoor* and red rose petals from the feet of the goddess, saying there was not sufficient time on my hands.

I needed to reach the hospital fast; there was no money on me. I hired a rickshaw. When I reached the Idgah hospital Rinki was not there. I rushed home and she was not there too. I went crazy, crazy with uncertainty crazy with apprehension. I was told that my aunt had come and taken her to her home so that on my return we could take Rinki to the widow who resided near her home. The widow lived under a tree in the temple premise. She did not charge money she did not speak. She was referred to as Mataji.

My aunt came searching for me. When we reached her home there was a crowd gathering, someone was whispering and the words fell on my ears. I can never forget that day. They were saying Rinki is no more. I jostled and shoved my way in and showered the *sindoor* and petals on Rinki. Just like the priest had told me I was not to touch them. I had collected them in my sari *aanchal* and now I had in one deft tug sprinkled them. She woke up with a start, and then she began to cry like one possessed.

We rushed her to Mataji's. She flung my daughter's arms wide. Placed a half cut lemon, clove and camphor on her palms and lighted earthen lamp on it. After one hour you will not believe that the girl we had carried to the temple a corpse came out walking back home. That is why she is the dearest to me. I get goose bumps when I remember those days. Rinki had transformed and morphed into 3 forms. Her face and lips became jet black her nails blue, her arms went yellow and her legs and feet turned black completely stiff and stone-like.

Hospitals fleeced us of money but the one who resurrected her, Mataji did not charge a penny. There is a Sai darbar and one Kali ji temple in the premise. Women converge there in the evening singing praises of the lord. When Bengali asked her how much money we owe, Mataji said *bhagwaan paisa mangta hai kya*, does the god ask for money? If that is what you wished then you should have taken her to the hospital. You see Bengali did not know much about her and her pristine ways. I am not a very religious person but since that day I follow her ruling of *no chadhawa no dikhawa* – no offerings no splurging.

There are some who say the goddess has come to reside in them. They behave like one possessed. The whole community would line up to them all elders shall crawl up to her and say *matarani* excuse me pardon me my sins they touch her feet they conduct prayers the husband can be seen asking for forgiveness. What sham what scam I say. There are so many pious people doing *tapasya* doing severe and strict penance but the god's or the goddesses never come to inhabit with those noble souls. Whereas, on the other hand here we see mere mortals, get to be possessed by the goddess, at strategic moments, every few years?

That is why during the chaitra Nauratri she continues one can come across lemon *sindoor* clove and flowers on some crossings and road intersections, offerings made to appease the goddess. Mataji is still living in the temple she has become feeble but is very renowned.

Nauratri which falls in the Hindu lunar month of *chaitra* that is to say sometime around march april is devoted to *Ma Kaali*. It is observed during the *shukla paksha,* the waxing phase of the moon, from new moon to full moon, which can be interpreted as leading from darkness to light. This darkness is also very figurative when compared with the dark tinge of *Kaali devi*. These nine days are dedicated to the nine forms of goddess Shakti. The beginning of this Nauratri marks the start of the Hindu New Year. This lunar based calendar is mentioned as *Vikrami Samvat*, founded by emperor Vikramaditya of Ujjain and is 56.7 years ahead of the prevailing solar Gregorian calendar. For example the year 2015 coincides with Vikram Samvat 2071-72.

Hindu *sanskaar's* say that *mundan* or the *chudakaran* is the child's first tonsure ceremony. It is usually done in the first year since birth or if not performed in this duration then in the third year. Only a tuft at the crown is left in some cases. Traditionally nose or ear piercing is also undertaken during these auspicious days. Marriages are never performed during these 9 days of festivity. The festival has great value and recognition as one's wishes desires and prayers are known to be answered. Ask and you shall receive, it goes without saying that any untoward inappropriate or obstinate is eschewed. Because Kali ji was angered she went on a rampage bloodthirsty. Afraid it would lead to the deluge the god's asked Shankar ji to contain her fury.

On the other hand Maha Nauratri are the 9 days celebrated during the bright fortnight of the month of *Ashiwin* coinciding with the advent of the winter and during september october. Each day is dedicated to the manifestation of the various forms of *Ma Durga*.

Pratipada: to Shailputri, colour of the day is Grey

Dwitiya: to Chandra Darshan Brahmacharini, colour of the day is Orange

Tritiya: to Sindoor Tritiya Chandraghanta Pujan, colour of the day is White

Chaturthi: to Kushmanda, colour of the day is Red

Panchami: to Skandamata, colour of the day is Royal Blue

Shashthi: to Saraswati awahan Katyayani Pujan, colour of the day is Yellow

Saptami: to Saraswati Puja Kalaratri Pujan, colour of the day is Green

Ashtami: to Durga Ashtami Mahagauri Pujan, colour of the day is Peacock Green

Navami: to Sidhdhidatri Puja Durga Visarjan, colour of the day is Purple

Dashmi: the tenth day is celebrated as Dussehra or Vijayadashami.

Goddess Durga is worshipped during the festival. Married womenfolk fast and pray with great devotion knowing that her prayers shall be answered by the benign goddess. Sour and astringent foodstuff is completely avoided. Some do severe penance by fasting without drinking water, some just by chewing on clove, some by avoiding grain in all forms in their diet, some cook food without sprinkling salt while some use rock salt, some feed on fruits some on fast-food available at shops and stores during these days.

On the first day the idol of the Devi purchased from the market, is established either on an altar or on a low stool which is covered by red cloth with golden lacy border and embellishment. Before placing the stool the traditional design called *chowk* is made with wheat flour. A *kalash* the metallic urn is placed at the Devi's feet filled with water over which a coconut covered with red cloth and golden trimmings is placed. Another *kalash* is filled with water over which five mango leaves are placed. This is topped by a clay plate that acts as a cover over which raw rice is set and an earthen lamp is allowed to sit over this rice base. Clarified butter or *ghee* is used to light this lamp. Care is taken so that this lighted lamp shall burn continuously for nine days. *Jau* or barley seeds are sown in a clay pot or in a wicker basket, which is placed at the feet of the revered Devi.

On the seventh day these *Jauharein* now grown tender and ten or eleven inches in height with a pale greenish yellow colour resembling fluorescent green are taken to the Devi temple along with articles of *shringara* her sdornment. *Shringara rasa* is one of the nine *rasas* or emotions propagated. They being and engulfing a range of sentiments. Some of which are presented below,

love, encompassing adornment and beauty
joy, encompassing mirth humour absurdity buoyancy
wonder, encompassing curiosity and ambiguity
courage, encompassing confidence poise pride
peace, encompassing tranquillity serenity
sadness, encompassing compassion sympathy
anger, encompassing annoyance hostility
fear encompassing, apprehensive agonize
and disgust, encompassing despair desolation

Shringara means and manifests into love and beauty. To indulge oneself in gorgeousness and beauty of oneself, to appease ones partner and consort. After much distraught and rampant rife during seven days, Kali ji is stopped and contained by Lord Shiva. Hence *Kali Devi* is also offered articles of beautification to appease her so she may forget the hysterical and dress up for her beloved Shiva to surrender to love beauty and universe. Black bangles red bindi comb mirror ribbons and articles of beauty are offered to the Devi. Lore has it that the more *the jauharein* flourish the more prosperity and love is received from the goddess to those offering.

There are some ritual and rigorousness in following the fast too. A do and don't reckon that has filtered down the ages from generation to generation. Anything sour is never used. Morning and evening prayers are performed with commitment and without fail. Hence it is advised that only when one can perform with complete devotion should one establish the Devi. The infirm in mind and body plainly fold their palms in prayer with devotion or fast on the auspicious days of *ashtami or navmi* or on the first day. For seven days the goddess is invited by lightening of the lamp, for the battle with the demon ravaged for seven days. On the eighth day presents and sweets are offered to appease the goddess so that she may remain pleased delighted and content after devastation and destroy.

Goats were offered at the altar of temples to soothe the conflicting goddess. This offering of yesteryears is nowadays replaced with piercing of the ear and donating the goat to the Brahmin or any family with young children who can feed on its milk. Those who cannot spend much, mould goats made out of kneaded wheat flour and cut it in a symbolic gesture. They offer the deity according to their ability secure in the thought that each shall be bestowed with the same fervour without any kind of favour or favouritism.

Locating a pundit during these days is a huge task in itself, for the pundits at the temples and the ones who visit homes are busy strutting from one home to another conducting prayer service or conducting *paath*. They too are showered with clothing's sweets fruits and hefty *dakshina* monetary gifts by their patrons.

Her husband's elder brother Omkar conducted *this jagaran* by taking donations as it was beyond his means. It is believed that if one conducts the festival by bringing and placing the idol of the Devi at home, it has to be conducted for three consecutive years. Family friends and relatives came for the nights of revelry. Singing devotional songs in praise of the goddess and offered coconut. When the coconut presented by Omkar was offered by breaking it at the idol feet it was found to be rancid time and again. That is when Budhaa intervened and asked her son to stop arranging these *jaagaran's* at home. She had consulted the pundit and he had told her plainly that these jagaran's should be held with proper and great concern and decorum. If not then they can be very risky Aarti concluded.

Males of all ages are known to perform great penance with utmost devotion. They visit the temple 21 days in advance to register with the pundit one kg or five kg or 21 kg of iron, as is deemed possible by them without burdening themselves. The pundit ensures that that much amount of iron in the form of nails rods or tridents is offered as prayers to the Devi over 21 days. The 21st day coincides with the final day of the Nauratri.

Drummers are called and a procession begins late at night to cover the distance upto the temple by morning. Much singing of hymns and dancing by devotees is conducted.

At each road crossing between the house to the temple, the mother or a lady member of the male performs a small prayer and leaves aside beetle nut leaf over which whole *supari* acer nut and lime along with camphor clove and *sindoor* powder are placed to appease the goddess. This lady shall also sweep the path for her son to travel, with her sari *aanchal*. He takes an early bath and shall wear unstitched clothes. He shall cover the distance by bowing low on the ground. Chanting of *Kali Ma ki jai* pierces the ambience at regular interval. Some men and women appear highly possessed and need to be placated.

Aarti's first born was suffering from cracks on his feet with blood oozing from them. When her elder sister suggested that she do penance at the feet of Kali ji Aarti the one with a modern outlook did not pay heed. You see this Kali ji is not one to remain in harmony, if the thought has occurred she shall take her pound, recollected Aarti. So even though I laboured and spent money like a swift stream on the doors of hospitals and doctors my son was not cured. When the problem persisted her sister decided to do penance on her behalf.

She offered to sow *jauharein* to appease her goddess so as to cure her son of his misery. She also made her penance harsher by pledging to cover the distance to the temple by lying down in devotion every inch of the path. So on the first day she sowed *jau* in a terracotta pot with her wish to be adhered to by Ma. When conducted with complete devotion these shall grow tall and swaying. Lots of hygiene and severity is to be performed, so rich people do not conduct it themselves but ask for their pundit to observe the fast on their behalf.

Her son was cured. She then remembered that he was sought by praying to the goddess. Henceforth most of his milestone days were commenced by offering prayers here. When he married we took out the procession from the temple and I also brought my daughter in law Aarti to this temple of the Devi. I asked her just one thing before selecting her; you shall have to live within the means of your husband's earnings? I did not take a thing from her parent's just give me your girl. Budhaa is very upset with me for my actions. She says I have married my son into the poverty stricken. She does not see the merits of the girl she assesses on different parameters. She may not reside in Kanpur but the younger Aarti is her ears and eyes keeping her informed of every move.

World over women are known to adopt and adept to the home they marry into the moment they marry and enter it, considering them-selves to be an integral part of it to the extent that they then bear the beatings the crudity the cruelty without a word or whisper. They patch up the gaping hole in the quilt of their married life with ease. No one teaches them these lessons but they all do so in all walks of life in all cities countries religions and decree. The degree of humiliation can be varied in their intensity and range. They may be physically visible or the unseen hurt of humiliation, that can be initiated by the husband or other members of the family or the family as a whole. How deplorable can such a family unit be called. The beasts also have some rules they apply and follow. They are always upfront, they like a good chase and killing. Never will they lurk as foe under the cloak of friends or family.

When Aarti was busy with her work at marriages, unknown to her, her younger sister Babli was being lured into her family by her mother in law and her *devar*, her husband's younger brother Rajkumar. He was a very good looking male. Too late she got to know of her sister's involvement. Who refused to see any blemish whatsoever in the family she was married into? Suffice to say that I stand corrected in my earlier observation that women gain acceptance of their new home and family on arrival. They evaluate and accept it first in some cases and then proceed to consider the rest.

While I was busy with taking marriage bookings I was not aware she was spending much time with my children on the insistence of my mother in law. She, who by now had got to know that a neat amount was stacked in Babli's name by my father, Kanpur as you shall learnt later was undergoing great social political and economic upheavals. The once flourishing township was to find itself stripped of all, law order economy. Money was scarce all around. Mills were shutting down as a result and men were without secure jobs. Babli was easy prey.

So Babli would not listen to any she refused to see the obvious she considered her sister of leading a pleasant life with nice people. The little bit that was uncovered by Aarti for her benefit was protested at vehemently. She was the encumbering imposing sister who did not wish to see her happy. She was made out to be the villain in her smooth running commentary of an idyllic life-match ahead.

Her brother's wary of finding a suitable match and family to marry her into gave in to the slips of rejection they encountered. Literally covered under heaps of taunts they silently bore from their spouse they readily agreed to marry her to the boy of her finding and choice. When Aarti protested that we sisters are different in mettle and that they should consider considering of the matter again they waved their hands in disappoint and disdain from the elder sister. Do you know how much time and money we have incurred on her with no result, they quipped at her nitwit?

On the other hand, when her in laws faced her with the desire to bring home her sister as bride for their youngest son, she stated matter of factly that bringing home her sister was out of question. That is when the family put their brains together to overcome her impede and imposing character. They concluded that one sister needed to be put forth and pitted against the other. The most ancient tactic that procured sought after results of winning always was utilised. Use the less advantaged to face the mighty with disparagement and disregard. Divide and rule to get the desired results without disaster.

Faced with much deceit and defeat she gave in to the demands of her sister with grudge. But not before issuing the Warning to all concerned parties. To her husband and his brother she said it's your calling and under no circumstance was she to be held responsible for the misgivings the sister who appeared so dear incurred, if any she appended appropriately.

To her sister she sternly reprimanded it was entirely her decision that she was marrying into the family she herself was married into. On no count, under any circumstance she underlined was she to approach her with issues she may have with any. Also she wished it to be known to all relations, family, friends and neighbours that she had not sought after this proposal for her.

To her in laws she laid down the congruent rules again. Geometry she had not learned but it appeared she was stating the corollary. Under no condition were they to come up to her with complain and quarrel. Simple, secure and most precise.

To her brothers and their wives she said, was one sister so unmanageable and unwieldy that they were shoving her to her hell with intent.

She felt like Abhimanyu surrounded by the victorious and gaming, encircled within a gamut of lies and vice. Abhimanyu was the illustrious son of the mighty Arjuna and nephew of lord Krishna. He was killed on the thirteenth day at the Kurushetra war. Once she relented she went down with not much of a fight unlike Abhimanyu, aghast at the ways of the god. The glees of the victorious doubled at seeing the untainted and perfect lose. She smiled inwardly at the prospect of the outcome, she who knew and understood that the game has just begun, that the results of the competition would be in her favour. It was but a battle lost the war consequence would declare the ultimate winner. Time to wait and watch for the day for that awaited result.

I knew that expenses shall be incurred in her marriage. I knew that we brothers and sisters were all with children now and expenses of our own. I knew that we would not be able to sustain the expenditure. I knew that the money in Babli's name needed to be kept aside for her. Thus I acted in her favour and swept the money in another account, for her aspirations and needs and wedding. Also to ensure that it does not fall in wrong hands. Also to scuttle any attempt to fleece my sister after marriage.

Prediction is a trait which follows the curve. A rising trend shall continue to ascend even after the variables are locked and on the other hand a drooping tendency shall show a downhill slide on shutdown. My mother in law's arch foretold that the girl was being lured for marriage with the purpose of money. As soon as she got word of the money being siphoned she demanded why have you removed the money from your sister's account?

It's not in your entitlement now to ask this question. It's my family prerogative to do as we deem correct. Only after her marriage can you ask about her welfare I had interjected softly but firmly. She could do nothing but whine like one hurt in the jungle chase. The prey was within reach but the pursuit did not allure any longer. The invitations had been sent so there was no going back, for her.

Time will test and time will tell she rued to herself. She who knew both the parties and their failings too well was agitated at the union. She who could foresee the future of both involved families. It was she who was teased and taunted by all, of being the sceptical one. She who loved her sister more dearly than all siblings put together, but none understood it. Marriages are made in heavens she tried hard to calm herself with the adage. She who had stood up for her sister as a warrior now stood defeated and dulled in spirit. She who went through the motions of the marriage with a heavy stone tied to her heart. It was she who curbed her feelings of anxiousness and anxiety, during the actual ceremony. It was she who went about the process of marriage with abandon. Who am I to deflect the happiness of my sister? If so be it so be it.

There were times when my relations with my mother in law have deteriorated to the point of no return there have been times when it has been pushed to the brink but each time it has endured and retraced its feet back to normalcy. Like two ally's we have remained like the carbon copy attached to the sheet. One cannot do without the other. At times when she was unwell and I was not on speaking terms with her it was I who would haul her up into the rickshaw and got her examined by the doctors. Purchased her medicines and laid her back in the bed. Fed her food and administer the medicines. I did all this without uttering a word directly to her.

She has subdued now and goes about harping and heaping my praises to all behind my back. She knows that she was and never shall be cared for as much as I have for her. The food she desired I cooked for her, the clothes she wished I brought for her. I still do. But our relation was volatile show it some heat and it shall flare to consume all in its way. We both understand this. Suffice to say some very good times also we have shared together. Occasions of picnics by the *ganga* / ganges, marriage birth birthdays and festivals.

Sooner than she thought, crisis occurred in the newly married couple's life. Her mother in law, who was unable to get even with Aarti with her protective husband by her side, knew which bolt needed to be tightened so that it squeaked the most. One battle one son she had lost but vowed to herself when the marriage vows were being conducted, that this one battle this son, take it in writing 'Ramawati had won'. In a matter of saying she corrected herself for she did not know to read or write.

Problems soon cropped in. We were as different as chalk and cheese. She was the youngest and most pampered. She had not learnt the ways of taking pride in work. Where I could endure she zapped. Where I thrived in working hard she lingered and lamented. She was devoid of the guardian who would ably hold her hands and guide and groom her during her adolescent years.

Scheming robbing cheating looting thugging thrived. Family members and friends waylaid and entrapped their victims with complete vivaciousness by laying trap and scooting with the easy cash. Like dacoits thugs were prevalent during the earlier centuries in India. They were suppressed by the British in 1830's. But now it seemed the footprints which remained latent were becoming visibly present in the dna of its citizens again. The people of Kanpur have a Nawabi attitude like the people of Lucknow. Lucknow can be given the benefit of having being host to Nawabs. But Kanpur just 85 km away reflected much in such ad-hoc glory, was to become a cesspool of corrupt and crime.

Circumstances may aim to change it; attempts to corrode it may affect it to some degree, seemingly. But try as much as one wants to augment and amplify the harshness of the situations by oppress, the dna of a person remains intact and inheriting. Mend it bend it tend it lend it send it or end it, but the dna shall append itself to you like the day to the night.

So if there are those that oppress there is an equal amount that shall come forward to liberate. Societies flourish and prosper in this state of equilibrium. Shift the balance and autocorrecting procedures ideally mushroom. When and where the auto-correcting gets crushed and routed then and only then the society shall fall prey to autocracy. Ramawati gained in strength by exploiting this facility to the hilt. Everyone was subjugated till they towed her line. She did not learn physics nor did she show any interest to learn by example, that everything in the world had a yielding point.

When one tries to pluck a flower some yield easily while with others one may have to struggle twist turn or tug the twig. Her younger sister bore well the conniving ladies wrath and scheming attitude with fortitude. I did not interfere and she did not complain. Years passed by and as long as I was staying in the house she felt protected albeit by an invisible arm. After I left she carried on like an injured soldier but without the assurance of her partner what could she achieve. Till one day I got a call from her in Delhi. Enough she lamented. I can take it no longer the son shall always remain her son and never transform into my husband.

You see, as long as I was with the family and later in Cantt area she was cared by my undetectable presence and hand that ably supported her albeit indirectly. Once I left for Delhi things took a bad turn. Determined she knew it was time for some action now. It was high time and the cause for the creaking bolt needed to be clinched.

Immediately she requested to be given a day's leave. She boarded the train at night and reached Kanpur early in the morning. Kanpur formerly (Cawnpore) is situated on the banks of the Ganges River. It's the 5th largest city in India by land area and the 75th largest city in the world. It was the industrial hub of northern India and was known as the Manchester of the East. Also known as the *Leather City* for it contains some of the finest tanneries in the world. Lore has it that the city was named after the warrior of Mahabharata Karn. Its roots can be traced further back to the Ramayana too.

At a distance of twenty five kilometres from Kanpur is the old city of Bithoor. Legend says that when Rama expelled Sita, she came here to sage Valmiki's religious retreat called ashram. Her twin sons Luv and Kush were born here.

It is believed that Sir John Burney Allens established textile mills and tanneries here late in the 19th century. By the beginning of the 20th century Lala Kamlapat Singhania and Sir J P Shrivastava established the JK Industries and the New Victoria Mills respectively. The Jaipuria family bought Swadeshi Cotton Mills and in 1928 Sardar Inder Singh founded India's first steel re-rolling mill at Singh Engineering. Ordnance Factory, Kanpur is the manufacturer of the Nirbheek meaning fearless revolver. The first light weight revolver weighing half a kg, exclusively for women.

When she reached home she saw her deserted sister sitting in the open *maidan* the park, for her in laws had shoved her out the previous night in the dark. She sat there alone and desolate quivering. I took her into a tight embrace and rose above the ashes Phoenix like. Ready to wage any battle any war on her behalf. Blood is thicker than water they say, adjoin to it some injustice and I can be your frontrunner.

I raged with the fire of anger indomitably to destroy any who would cross my path now. Determined I entered the house with Babli and questioned Sashi and Meena our sisters in law. The two said she works slowly. So what roared Aarti possessed. The whole family had descended by now. She is not denying work. You do not feed her do not talk to her with the respect she deserves, her husband abandons her yet she slogs for all. So what she works unhurriedly but she does not work deliberately. So what, do you think you can heap atrocity on her? So what. she trailed off saying I gave them in pucca Kanpur style.

What style I enquired. Kanpur style UP style she appended. And what is that if I may ask so. Leave it you shall not bear to listen such words. Oh come on I chided give me a sample. But remember you asked for it. Okay I nodded prudently. The writer in me wanted all as it transpired. The me in me was sending caution signals. I wondered how bad or worst can some play-acting be. I was wrong. It was a bad judgement said the 'me' later, but a far-sighted one said the writer.

For the next moment she turned around to face me. She stood tall and stern. She rolled up her sleeves and in chaste UP style Hindi was using the f and the b words. One sentence and I was covering my ears astounded. She was unstoppable. She did not seem to see the 'me' cringe or the writer-me aghast as she gushed on, at the feeble voice I could hear for she was in her element and was being very loud. God bless anyone who takes *panga* umbrage with you I said with a smile, just so that she is pleased with her performance when she calmed down and collected herself. I did not want her to feel she was taken for a ride; else she would not be as candid as any judge's sentence.

Our parents are no longer alive I am not living in Kanpur why do you want to chuck her out now. She stressed on the word now. Why, answer me. Where shall she go? Her husband Rajkumar kept repeating just one sentence in one tone, I shall not leave her I shall not leave her. My husband Bengali kept saying, either way, just finish the issue once and for all. My overarching argument was that if you do not wish her to be around let the couple go together. So I kept uttering let go of both; one should not let go of her on her own. Suddenly they were all speaking at the same time. None seemed to appear as listening to the other's point of view. Each was intently harping its own tune.

The crux of the matter was that before she could question anyone in detail her mother in law stood up tall ahead of her and flaring her arms about her shrieked aloud take her away take her away then folding her palms in pity lamented I'll remarry my son just take this woman away just take her away. That sight is printed on my mind like *shlokas*, the holy verses engraved on the temple walls.

Patiently Aarti spoke to her, and then it shall be a case of a case. 'Case' hereby referring to being the 'police case' in our context, in case one is not completely conversant with the terminology used locally. No she declared no case etc shall be allowed in this home as long as I am alive. Just simply take her away, take her away. Where to I demanded where to? Where to I don't care, take her with you or take her to your brothers she confronted. In that case we shall put up a case. Okay who is afraid of court and cases challenged the mother. She was under the impression that I could not be away from my work for long. During my absence she would tackle the 'case' as she wished, in her favour.

You want me to take her away you disappoint me dear mother in law for that is just what I wished and came here for. You have paved my way with ease. Such a great opportunity you have lost of creating a grand *tamasha* of strewing obstacles in our path. Also remember you have not left an iota of way for her return when you disowned and dislodged her at the darkest hour of the night. The men of this house listen you are all bangle wearing cowards to align yourself to her illogical demand.

I asked my sister I'll interfere only when you pledge total alliance with me. You shall not ask or question me my doings and undoing's. In my neighbourhood I am known to bring many a callous and erring husbands to their senses. I have picked up the cane and slogged at men who have had the tenacity to hit their hapless wives. Rescuing battered women and of taking them to the hospital for their treatment. I learnt to care for the ill and infirm at the hospital.

Then I proceeded to the haughty Ramawati. Again I ask you, you want her gone fine, but let the two go together. No she replied unperturbed and decidedly. My son shall not leave the threshold. Okay then hold on to your son. Still, three more times I asked her the same but she did not relent. In fact she was pouring oil to fire by saying take her away I shall marry my son again. That was the last straw. Her singsong continued like a woman possessed. You lark I'll teach you a lesson I swore inaudibly to myself, one that shall make you forget singing.

Families disagree amongst themselves families fight families brawl. *Kuch bhi karne se pahle faisle parr nazar dalte hain. Aage chal ke achcha hoga ki achcha nahi hoga.* Before doing anything one must put a cursory glance over the decision of their action. Would it be right or would it be wrong in the long term. I may be unlettered but don't know from where I know all the rules and regulations. It's all there in my head. She illustrated her acumen with flair.

She asked her sister to pack whatever she needed to take with herself. Just my children she had muttered. So within no time we were out of the house. My sister did not as much as look back to glance around. Why would one want to keep the memory of a jail house for remembrance sake? I do not remember any convict shown looking back longingly at the jail on release, in any released film.

Straight away we went to the police station, there we registered her complain and put forth our application – she actually used the word application. In my home town there is only one rule one anthem, money it is called. So I shoved a tidy amount and made a strong complain, a little exaggerated one you see. When I looked up at her she sighed at my naive attitude. It's always so she explained, otherwise why would anyone care to move their butt for an in-fight or family brawl. Like most defaulters Budhaa knew it would be in her best interest to remain quiet and not interfere with the proceedings or influence them.

That is when Rajkumar went delirious with panic at the thought of Babli leaving him. He snatched the interrogating papers and pen and threatened to tear them apart. I knew that the whole exercise would prove to be futile if such a thing were to happen. So I went up to him and gave him a strong shrug. He stood there stunned for sure. When your mother does not give proper meals to your wife you turn a blind eye and become a crackpot. Now again you turn and behave like an idiot on demand. Saying so, I snatched away the official papers to my relief.

This turn of events became too much for the mother to handle. She pleaded and whined *bhaiyya* take her away. The children shall stay here said the son knowing that his wife would return for the daughters. Take them away scorned his mother. They remain here said the son. Oh too much mushiness at this moment became unbearable for me. So I gestured at the Inspector. Taking my cue he thundered let the girls decide. They said they would like to remain with their mother, wise girls, my blood I beamed inwardly.

Years ago when I came back from Etawah after the marriage assignment of a patron's daughter, completely exhausted yet elated by the profits I had made. I got to know of the changed scenario at home and my in laws intentions. The whole situation was cooking behind my back and I did not have a figment of its occurrence. The surprise they pulled on me was embittering and rendered me disillusioned. The first thing I did was that without the knowledge of anyone I transferred the money from Babli's account with the knowledge of my siblings in my account. To safeguard my sister's interest.

The previous night before leaving Delhi for Kanpur I spoke to my elder sister then alive and asked her to look for an accommodation for the younger one near her locality. I went and met my contacts and secured a job as ayah for her at a school. Her children were also to be enrolled in the same. Then I went to the police station and deregistered the severe complaint with them, without anyone's knowledge. You see, we have our daughters and sons to be married off and no one ever became famous by washing their dirty linen in public. Would it not amount to sacrilege and acting carelessly on a parent's part nor would it bring any glory to the family whatsoever.

When the court proceedings for their separation were initiated, all members went along with the diktat and the decree with a great degree of effortlessness, like a sharp knife on cheese smooth till the very end. There was not a voice of disagree dissent dispute or differ. I cautioned each member of the family to sever ties with my sister. I warned them loud and clear that none were to convene or converse with her. If I get to know that someone is trying to mend the bridge we sever today they shall be my worst enemy, beware! Thus secured happily in her new life she worked hard for herself and her two daughters.

Many such cases were coming to light. Many well to do happy families were reduced to penury and plight. Bonhomie was replaced by bitchiness and blame. Families upon families were on the verge of havoc and hackneyed. It appeared a silent epidemic was gripping the city. Like always the lowest strata of the society was reeling under its effect firstly and formerly. The middle and high class remained aloof by the contagion comfortably cocooned in their snugness.

Who can harness a determined blaze which just needs an obliging wind to blow in its direction? Within no time the city stood paralysed and plagued by the socio-economic factors engulfing each class and every ethnicity. One needs to better understand the combination and its influence on how a progressive society headed towards stagnation and regress.

On 25 June 1975, the then President of India Shri Fakhruddin Ali Ahmed, declared and imposed a state of nation-wide Emergency on prime minister Indira Gandhi's recommendation, who cited national security as its cause. Curfew was imposed trade unions and rallies banned, the police reigned supreme with power to search without warrant seize and arrest at will.

Armed aided and encouraged by the laws the police grew totalitarian and tyrannical, oppressing any leader that seemed to rear its head up. Political leader's activists of all array, small medium or big were arrested and locked up in jails. Some leaders who had fought for the freedom struggle of India against the British Raj were rounded off by the police and jailed by the ruling native government; stark irony seemed to have befallen on them. While the former was a matter of pride this was no less, fighting against internal and domestic debauchery.

On one hand subjection and subjugation of trade unions and the people at large incapacitated the relations between them and the bosses that be. The industrial powers became fortified on the other hand. The Supreme Court and the courts were rendered debilitated. States ruled by opposition parties were declared to be governed by the President Rule. So states of Gujarat and Tamil Nadu came under the spell of this rule. The social media then comprising of the radio the Tv and the newsprint were curtailed by censorship. The moral illegitimacy fell on the government for not performing its responsibility and duty with accountability.

Power needs assuage not clout. When power comes people fail for they forget this dictum. They consider it a matter of eternality and attribute it a manner of forever, foolishly. Power like wealth resides at will; it's gossamer with frivolous fickle and flighty features. Power is akin to a staircase or ladder. The same set of steps and rungs shall take one ahead and these very rungs shall be the bearers of one's downward. The uphill task is onerous not many willing to extend that grip to pull you against the gravity. The downstairs has plenty seekers to drag any, gravity included.

General elections were called for May 1977, by the government reeling under hyped and biased information provided by the coterie. The amalgamated Janta Party was created by Indian political parties opposed to the State of Emergency. They won.

When the power scales tilted the disadvantaged trade unions reeling under months of clout-less-ness thought they could now reign supreme, and flouted their power. Flouted power suffers and so it disgraces the wielder. The police on the other hand who by now had set into the groove of absolute supremacy continued in exercising its power arbitrarily.

Riots resulted. Whereas the pre-partition riots had patriotism written on them and post-partition riots had communalism written on it, these were clearly the riots between the great divide, the rich-poor class initiated riots. Whereas the 1931 riots of Kanpur were religious sect originated but these nearly half a century apart were secular in category, these were what is popularly known as "class cleavage antagonism"

Now the outrageous question arises why did the fragile natured fleet footed power retain and remain with the police autocracies? The answer remains in the fact that it was protected and cosseted by the Law. So the Law of the land is paramount and needs governing bodies who are just and can on all accounts as well as counts adhered to it. Seems like a paradox, for sure. But with transparent governing and empowering of the judiciary a little headway seems to have made a dent to the old order. Sooner than later we shall have the rights of citizen's honoured and rightly blazing the path to a righteous society. I have a surreal feeling about that as I write the words. Do you?

Between the unions and the police the hackled and the hackneyed people stood ostracised. The mill owners pulled out of the city like an erupting volcano trying hard to empty its gut out. Like the one-way process of escape. With no hope and no scope for returning, leaving without a backward glance. When the going gets tough the tough get going, one can safely say is the rule businesses are governed by the world over.

The irony of ironies is that when she was near him he cared two hoots for her. Once gone her husband would be seen waiting at the school gates for her glimpse and pleading with her to come back. But the strings of desire were snapped secured snapped secured many a times and then ultimately snapped with finality, when the court injunction arrived. If he thought it was all a joke 'the snap's and 'the secures' he was really being juvenile. Well then the joke was definitely on him. Luck should never be pushed beyond a certain point, it retaliates. Hopefully he has learnt when to stop pushing one's luck harder.

No nut no bolt could secure the lines now. When Aarti got to know of his pursue she tutored her sister that she ask him to dole out money for their children. She also admonished her sister to never 'handover' herself to the brute ever. Handover, the word was used by Aarti and I write it verbatim. Surprised, well so am I.

There are times when the old lady gingerly hinted at bringing the two separated together. Aree, what is this you are speaking of now do not talk to me about this issue, I speak loud and clear shrilly. When we don't want to travel that path why harp of that route. What I failed to understand was that she was keeping count of each failed and futile encounter in her mind for future reference and seeking opportunity to be even. She was like the jungle ant-house, tranquil and composed looking from the outside, encasing much turmoil and chaos within from the viewer. Predatory in her approach, she was to be.

I remember earlier also I was called and asked to take my sister away. We brought her home and cared for her. She was completely bed-ridden for months. But her woes were not only because of her young age. When she felt the cramps she did not know what to do or understand of them. She nudged her husband but he said it must be due to the food she consumed. So when the cramps appeared again she would go to the toilet to ease off the pain. Tired and fatigued after some more trips and in much pain she called for her mother in law again. She said it's 2 o'clock now wait till the morning. On her next trip the child was born to her. Afraid alarmed and anxious she wailed out aloud her voice superimposing the tiny wail of arrival from the petite one.

My other brother in law Beeru rushed in and seeing the scene in front of him tore his shirt apart in a flash and picked up the child in the frayed garment. Babli lay on the floor crying and shivering with some apprehension some weakness some delight some relief, her pain gone.

3 o'clock we got the message of the new born. We rushed home and one sight one look at my pale sister and I knew that something was drastically wrong. If anything were to happen to my sister I wailed at her plight, I'll bang each and every brick of this house and its housemates to rubble, I threatened. My sister lay still. When she refused to move I knew she was hit by a paralytic stroke. Mother in laws drama began again when she learnt about her being rendered incapacitate.

Take her right-away she fumed take her right-away she fretted afraid if something were to happen she would be scoffed at by the neighbourhood. Wonder what right she had, to talk so, after taking away her right to dignity of labour. Right away we called for the rickshaw and that very instant we tenderly lifted Babli to take her home. It was a chilling winter night, the thick turbid fog that appeared to descend that night I have not experienced since. I love the winter months the most but some foggy nights still render me sleepless. Thoughts of stillness and the stillness of my sister abound to hound.

Affectionately we cared for her and I must say that Bengali allowed me to spend as much money as I needed to on her, on alternative treatments. I think two minor operations were also performed. Slowly she regained her strength colour and confidence. Whence Rajkumar her husband learnt about her recuperating, he began coming home and pestering *bhabhi* kindly send her home. How long could we let her be at our place too, so we sent her back with a heavy heart after counselling her to have a voice of her own.

When her second daughter was born I had relocated to Delhi. She would call me sometimes and tell me of mother in law's torments, I would tell her never mind, trudge along. Her problems again boiled down to money. Rajkumar under his mother's spell was accustomed to working erratically. He worked as a contractor for house building. Whereas his income was not appending much the household income then, it was substantial now. But he offered all the money to the old woman. It's not that my sister disapproved of this she just wished some of it to be handed to her too. But his going to work at will was becoming a major deterrent to the earnings. When he did not pay up mother in law deducted her food. Sometimes Babli asked her neighbours for food and at times for some money.

If only my elder brother was alive our family would be on a different trajectory. He was the ambitious one. After his school he would lounge about at Bada Chauraha, the great intersection, so to say. He had a tall personality and was a voracious speaker. The Janta Party needed young men to canvass for them. He was recruited, and asked to take a tempo a mike and verbalize about the Party agenda and mobilise a crowd to come and listen to their leaders speak. Since he was very articulate slowly he was given charge to get the pamphlets printed and decide on its matter, for he knew the public-pulse with alacrity. When the leaders gave their speeches he was the first to raise slogans in their favour. He was a frontrunner during Party processions.

He was beginning to have great clout with the peers police and party-men. He would lend a helping hand to any who needed redress. A battered wife an err-ing husband who needed to be straightened by showing him some muscle and law a widower with pension related delays a neighbourhood boy wrongly implicated and in police custody a house being demolished. The poor got monetary help from the Party for the marriage of their daughters and he guided young unmarried men who were hounded like dogs and sterilized to seek justice.

He asked me to inform of any sort of injustice by any in the neighbourhood. Soon I was convincing the oppressed to fight for their rights. I would accompany them to his Party office and get their complaints registered. Wherever possible he would assist the downtrodden get a fair deal from the concerned authority. Soon enough I was a permanent fixture at the office too, for word got around that I could get them out of their miseries. We were on a roll, just like school days, except with my elder brother now. There is so much injustice all around if one stops to listen and see, being part of the indiscriminating and liberating felt good felt great.

What happened to him I ask with prudence and care not wanting to rush her into territory where she did not feel secure to traverse? My father would tell us that when he was an infant my brother suffered from *kala bukhar* for which he underwent a spinal operation. The doctors had warned my father that he was very susceptible and would not lead a long life. During one of the cavalcade there was lathi-charge and he hurt his toe. That injury proved fatal for him. The fever was deep seated and spread in his veins she said. He lost his thick tuff next he lost enormous weight too. She was stating the symptoms.

Frightened we shifted him to the Medical college hospital at Lucknow. There we were informed that he was suffering from acute cancer. The word itself is anathema in our society. All anyone could offer was sympathy on learning of his condition. Strangely none offered prayers for they did not want him to suffer such to suffer much.

On the eighth day after Holi a big fair a *mela* is organised in Kanpur. It is said that Ram and Sita played Holi on this day in Kanpur on their way to Ayodhya on their return from Lanka after slaying Ravana. A huge procession is carried out and theatre person dressed as Ram and Sita are carried on open vehicles around town. I was married by then and we were celebrating with colours when we got word of his demise. He had chosen a day when the city was in harmony as he wished and in celebration and in procession. The same year can be attributed to the decline and demise of the Janta Party as well.

I find some ambiguity here in her tale. For we all know that for all practical purposes Ramchandra ji with Sita ji and his convoy began their journey after Dussehra and reached Ayodhya in 21 days. For the two festivals always fall 21 days apart. There is no way they could have celebrated Holi or the 8th day of Holi at Kanpur which is a spring festival, whereas Diwali is a winter festival. Kanpur and Ayodhya are at a mere distance of 215 kilometres. Since we are dwelling on Kanpur I am also reminded of the Postal Index Number of the city or the PIN code which happens to be 208-00x. Whereas, it's Subscriber Trunk Dialling / STD code is 0512.

Kala bukhar or black fever was a widespread tropical disease, it is also known as Kala Azar. The word Azar originates from Persian meaning fever. Annually it is said to affect 3 to 4 lakh people. Symptoms vary from fever anemia enlargement of the spleen and liver. Since the affected person's skin turns dark dull and grayish it was popularly known as Kala or Black fever. Some also call it the Dumdum fever. Its medical name is Visceral leishmaniasis (VL) caused by protozoan parasites. She said that the fever enters the bones. She was correct for it is known to affect and attack the bone marrow. The carrier of the disease is the innocuous sand-fly. Treatments include chemotherapy. She was right again for she said that he died of cancer. Chemotherapy and cancer are synonyms in India.

Now the mother in law rues that her son does not contribute to the running of the household expenses. That he provides for her and her children. Their children she corrects, when I look at her disapprovingly. She laments that he remains out most part of the day, with Babli. 'On my conditions' heaves a silent Aarti, did I not say so, at the outset 'On my terms'? If Aarti thought that her family 'wedding' woes were over, she could have been farthest in her estimate.

It's not that mother in law preferred me or favoured me. Does a leopard change its spots? She was the same with me. When my husband was working and giving her every single paisa, everything was hunky dory. If he refused or reduced some cash she would skip my lunch or maybe offer some dry *roti* only.

When my husband was unwell due to spine injury and was laid down in bed with pain and laid down from his job too. I clearly remember those days. One day in particular stands out, the day when I stood on the terrace and my infant son kept pointing at *the kulfi* – ice cream vendor crying uncontrolled. Bengali asked me why he howls so much, I informed him it's the *kulfi* he desires. The vendor went door to door with a red cloth tied over the pitcher placed on his cart, to attract his customers. Inside was a freezing mixture of ice and rock-salt. The salt was used to dip the temperature further. Ice as we all know begins to form at 4 degrees Celsius.

In this saline mixture was placed the small conical tin container filled with boiled thick milk sugar nuts and essence of the *kewra*. No artificial flavouring, (*Kewra* is Panadana syrup). The lid was secured tight and doubly protected by using bicycle tyre-tube rubber-band of two inch thickness. So that they secured on to the lid snugly, thereby ensuring that no salty water entered its contents. It would take him just 10-15 minutes to freeze a fresh batch.

He would deftly remove the cone from the pitcher; rub it between his palms so that the warmth loosened the freezing treat from its edges. Deftly he would scoop the *kulfi* using his knife, place it on a green circular leaf and cut it into 4 parts. Sprinkle some more *kewra* water and place a wooden spoon before handing the *kulfi,* that was creamy textured and tasted heavenly.

We did not have even a single rupee with us. Dejected at his condition he got up to go and collect some amount that was due. Half way through he spotted a shining white tin coloured coin lying by the culvert. He scooped down with pain to collect the coin hungrily. He turned it around to verify its value. To his amazement it was indeed a sterling one rupee coin, not the bad penny he assumed. He retraced his steps and searched for the vendor and brought the chilled *kulfi* wrapped in newspaper for the child. Then he went back contented to search for work and collect his dues, possibly.

That day stands out in our life as a milestone. That day Bengali was determined to seek work. We often remember that day and this which she related. Scarcity can tarnish the righteous when faced with adversity. I was buying a little milk from the milk vendor, don't know if the milkman added water to it but I would mix an equal amount of water before feeding it to my infant son.

Once when he came to collect his dues I was petrified as I had no money and he was known to be an abusive man, if circumstance demanded so. Fearing that a scene would be created in front of all I had but one option. When he asked for his payment I stood up to him erect and stridently said but I have already paid you your dues. Have you he wondered aloud. Yes yes don't you remember I pitched in.

Fearing and pleading inwardly all the time that he forgoes his calculations. Since I had a just image in the neighbourhood he swallowed his error or maybe pretended to err, maybe I have forgotten he said and turned away.

But soon enough my son fell ill we had to shift him to the hospital. My brother's helped me a lot financially. The vendor may have forgotten but I and my conscious can never forget the incident. We always remember and remind our children of it. For the lure of some we had to pay out enormous. Those were the days I had known fear. Those were the days I swore to earn to be financially independent.

Anyway I told my mother in law that we can make *genda* flower strings that are used by decorators for marriage and other functions. We need not step out of the house for this. We cannot just keep sitting by in the hope for work to drop in our laps we need to work. She agreed readily knowing that even a trickle would be welcome.

On the first day we asked the decorator for 20 kg flowers. He also provided us with the long needles and jute yarn. The full household chipped in enthused. We sorted the flowers according to their size and shade. We strung the flowers together; it felt like celebration time after months of gloom we rejoiced as we laboured. By evening we had earned a neat rupees sixty @ 3 rupees per kilogram. Soon we were earning 150 bucks. Each member got their share. My sisters in law could not believe their eyes when they were given their due. They who always wore dresses made from the mill cloth their father brought from the mill, for the very first time wore dresses of their choice. Self reliance is a windfall none can undo.

But this job had seasonal demands. So next we switched on to making paper packets crafted from old magazines. The size of magazine was much larger those days. We would get 40 to 50 kg paper from Parade bazaar. Make glue from flour and paste the edges with it and keep it aside for drying. Then we would make stacks of 1000 in assorted sizes of one kilogram half a kilogram and 250 grams. Bengali would make rounds of grocery shops and sell these bales. We were on our way to self sufficiency.

When guest arrived unannounced we would make black-gram pulse *kali masoor dal* kebabs quickly. Just soak the pulse for 10 minutes. Grind the pulse with ginger chilli in a mixer. Make small pancakes and shallow fry it. Then serve it hot with chutney she concludes. Lip smacking and delicious, it earned us many compliments.

She named a few items off hand. Samosa, moong dal salted Imarti, fermented maida sweet Imarti, Jalebi, chakli, khoye ki barfi, shahi paneer, kofta palak paneer, besan ki sabji, green pea rasajen, chicken Chinese with coconut milk, do pyaza mutton, roomali roti, chow mutton, fish rehu, khus khus prawns. I remember all.

We appended our income during national festivals, 26th of January and 15th of August. Really, I ask her the exuberance in my voice apparent to her as well as my being envious of her. To get to craft the National Flag, to me is a matter of great pride. Tell me in detail every aspect of it I insist more for my benefit than for the written word.

Preparations begin 2 to 3 months in advance. Firstly around 50 Kg of bamboo is purchased. Utilising an elongated knife it is cut to size by one while the other shall smoothen the frayed edges by filing them evenly with a penknife. The third shall stock them. Earnest work would start one month prior to the date of delivery. Again the family would pitch in with fervour. Saffron, green and blue colours along with white paper and cotton is purchased from the wholesale market. Since my brother was with the Janta Party he procured the central seal for us. They worked in tandem. They worked on an imaginary conveyer belt they worked with feverish concern. The family appeared united.

One would paint with cotton dipped in saffron shade and deftly colour the topmost band with it. The next would twist it upside-down and skilfully swab the green coloured cotton. The other would with great expertise stamp the circular spoke-wheel like seal on the central white band in blue. The fourth person would apply the homemade glue on to the side edge and roll it over the smoothened sticks. The fifth collected them when dried and made bunches of thousand then secured them with bands. One week before the event Bengali and his brothers would take the train to Delhi sell their ware at the Sadar bazaar and return by the evening train. Money, hard earned money was so much cause for celebration. It was party time for us.

We went to the circus at Arya Nagar. There we saw that they were selling water. We lived nearby we began selling potable water. Then I wondered if water is selling laddoos shall also sell and then if laddoos were selling so would the samosas. Three shows were conducted per day. It was raining coins. Even though the Mill was locked we were able to purchase fridge Tv wooden bed. Ramawati was happy.

Sleep eluded her. She was unable to focus. Work did not charm. Grandchildren a source for her joy were left abandoned. Her daughters rallied about her. Her husband carried on unperturbed. Zombie like she too carried on. Until the voices she heard all the time pursued her thought her bearing her being. Engulfed within the noises of the repetitive echo of the communication she overheard she succumbed. She felt overstrained and over burdened by them and surrendered in the face of peril. There was no escape none freedom from them the screeching. She was defeated for the first time she had lost a battle without giving it all her might. She had relented with a whimper. She had lost the game before it had begun.

Like a Black hole she was collapsing within, unable she was to contain and sustain herself. Darkness and drudgery was all she perceived about her. Dismal and dismay abounded. It appeared that an electron had lost its energy to sustain itself in its designated state of equilibrium and orbit.

A)

Wounded beyond the tensile strength of the character she displayed she yielded. 8, the number eight did not bode well for her she said. She was the eighth born. Her family that was prosperous and on the path of well-being was afflicted by problems, she had overheard her parents say so when they thought she was beyond their hearing.

B)

On her 8th year running disaster had struck when she was pulled out of school by her mother, her first endeavour at work a permanent source of joy and income wrapped within moments notice.

C)

On the 8th of a month she failed to remember, on the day of the holi celebrations, she got her first memorable thrashing from her mother who could not sustain being irritated time and again by her. When, she had unknowingly spoilt, the sweets with colour. The incident always manages to creep up when she is preparing sweets.

D)

Her daughter fell gravely ill on *Janamashtami*, the eighth day of the dark fortnight of the month of *Shravan.* Lord Krishna whose birth is celebrated with great fervour on this day, was the eighth avatar of the protector lord Vishnu.

E)

On the 8th day of the birth of her third grandchild she was to overhear her husband speak lovingly on the phone, unaware she was home. She also discovered his flattery from the taped recordings. The twosome had disintegrated. The strings that tugged at her heart slackened at that very instance. No music could ever be played or set to tune on them again.

F)

On the 8th day she received a call that chilled her nerves. Her daughter had gone back to her husband's home with her new born son. The weather was chilly and the change of place was attributed to the temperature the child was running. He was not responding to any treatment.

F1)

They had brought the child home earlier than expected. For, she had heard the notorious tales of new babies born going missing from the hospital premises. Once the child was born she did not let the child away from her eyes. If statistics were of any measure of measuring then they stared pointedly at her. Eight girls were born that day and just one boy. *Krishna Khaniyya* said the nurses and rallied about her and the new born.

She who had worked at the hospital knew all about the ways that were to be known as to how these wards were run. She had left for Kanpur immediately. She shifted the child to the large medical at the outskirts of Lucknow. She fought with the authorities and doctors that the child be given attention and care. She the unlettered one had carried each and every record and reports of the child. It helped them to go for tests and diagnosing better. It was a case of poisoning. She did not believe them. She showed them his photographs. The child had taken ill on the train journey. The daughter then recollected they had poured some hot tea purchased from an unauthorised vendor to warm the chilled milk. She had given some to the elder son who took a sip and threw it, saying it tasted filthy. He too had taken ill but soon recovered.

That was when she came to know about the racket by illegal vendors who were using white paint in lieu of milk. Lead content leading to the toxic nature of the tea. When she was asked to sign some forms she informed she could not read or write. The doctors appreciated her efforts and her willingness to spend money like water. They said they have seen the richest of the rick back off when it came to spending money on the ailing. They saluted her spirit her verve.

Fate repeats incidents in a cyclic manner too. As an infant she too had consumed the lethal oil. It was the erudite clerk called *munshi* who asked for a live demonstration by the infant. True to her nature she had snuggled up to the food stuff scattered and promptly fed on it. Her father was spared in the court of the law. She was also reminded of one of her earliest memories. Memories of her childhood days when unknowingly she had fed chilled milk to the toddler Maya. Days, when she was still Munia, days when Aarti had not emerged.

Cyclic event reminded her that like her father she too hurt her eye, when the pressure cooker burst. Cooked *chana dal* pulse was splattered over her face. She lost her vision for three months. No medication helped. She was directed to see an elderly doctor Pahwa of Delhi who was visiting Kanpur. With his treatment she regained her sight.

E1)

It was my call to her. Call from her saviour as she puts it, the clutching onto the last twig for subsistence. Reassurance followed by her resurrection from the ashen. She gathered her spirits and *dupatta* tightly around her waist, at ease now, the voices now having seeped out of her. The child a blessed one.

D1)

The lord who protects saved her daughter's life maybe on goddess deity Lakshmi's insistence, who is his consort.

C1)

She had known then there are limits to everything. If one wished to lead a strong successful life the middle path needed to be toed. Excess is damaging.

B1)

Her waywardness had given way and directed her to her acceptance by the Marwari family.

A1)

She had often wondered as to why her parents did not accede to the medical treatment for curtailing the production of babies. In her eyes it was the foremost and sore reason for her family's calamity and disintegration.

Anyway, in all the above cases, what initially appeared as calamity failure debacle was indeed the boon of the god's that came her way. At the time they occurred they were grouse and gross. They shook her world of calm with catastrophe. But months into the occurrences she would be grateful to them and their incurring.

Those were tough days for her, she could barely make both the ends meet or provide one square meal to her three children. So when she learned that she was in family way again she baulked. She approached her husband with her suggestion to abort the child; he got very agitated at her sacrilege suggestion. Dare you do any such thing he warned her. Not one to give up so easily she called upon her sister in law to come along with her to the hospital. They under the complete spell of their mother and her mother in law heaped profanities on her. It's a sin they hollered. How can you even think on such lines? Don't include us in your immoral act.

Hapless she approached her mother to escort her to the hospital; she who was warned by her son in law about her daughter's insane claim diplomatically insisted that the matter rests between the two of them. Her husband had used whatever little contacts he had to find out the procedure and the regulations involved. He knew that the doctors would not consider her unless he signed the papers.

As last resort she cajoled her own brother's wife to come along with her. She declined worrying at the social stigma attached to the act.

She found the attitude of her family pathetic. She found the strutting husband pitiable, his swagger was due to the fact that the rules stated that the husband accompany the wife and sign the papers for the procedure.

Such callousness and insensitivity she could not understand. The world was progressing exponentially but these people wished to remain unorthodox and rooted to bigoted beliefs in the name of tradition? Their behaviour spurned her to be more determined. She took her youngest in her lap and approached the hospital alone. She dressed up in a pale sari removed her earrings and bangles except for one in each arm starved a little and appeared unkempt.

All this elaborate makeup was done to assume an old and haggard look. She approached the peon at the OPD and declared she wished for an abortion. Everyone who heard her was taken aback. When the authorities got to know of the morning debacle at the hospital they sighed, there we are spending lacs on promotions and awareness with practically no results and here come this lady all on her own asking for the needful. She not only demands she insists she would create a great ruckus if her plea was not heeded to.

Curiosity got the better of all nurses and doctors. Take her history retorted one of them pleased. Pen and a type written form in hand a lady doctor approached her for consultation and guidance.

Name: right away she lied and supplied with a false name.

Married: yes

Husbands name: false name supplied

Address: false address given without a thought

Children: 6

But Aarti I butted in you have 3 children, she cut me short *arre* when all info is false then to put weight-age to my case I decided these people would care when I furnish them with my plight of one too many. As it is when you have restored to telling white lies then whether it's single or many, how does it matter I mock prodded her claim. It was a sensitive matter but it was long done and over so we could indulge in a little jollity without being critical.

Husband's job: that is when the real drama began. Wiping the nonexistent tear with her tattered sari *pallu* she sobbed in it aloud to gain a larger audience. That whimper of a man he does nothing but while away his time drinking binging beating up his family. Such a large family we have and not any money or food to feed the tiny mouths. Each day is a misery each moment a dread. Tell me how I can think of another child in such a pathetic condition as mine. Today too he does not accompany me must be lying in some ditch.

Soon word got around that the doctor's had agreed to go ahead with the abortion and surgery. Happily she arrived home and informed her husband that on such a date she would get rid of the unwanted foetus. I have never done a thing without informing my husband she proclaimed. Right or wrong I have told all to Bengali, I implore behind the back activities. Bengali did not pay heed to her uttering's for real. For he was comfortable in the fact that come what may, without his signature nobody would dare admit her to the hospital.

Two days prior to reporting to the hospital she took her youngest and went to her mother's place. There she left the baby in her mother's care and on the pretext of meeting with her childhood friends went straight to the hospital to complete any formalities. Soon she was back. Early morning the next day her mother was upset to see her leaving again. Aarti casually told her I'll just be back. At least eat some breakfast before going implored her mother. Just going to conduct some tests at the hospital mother don't know if it's advisable to eat she furnished.

It so transpired that Bengali was escorting his married sister to her home when he happened to pass by the very hospital in question. Immediately he had an urge to visit the hospital for this was the stipulated day Aarti had informed him of the surgery being conducted. His sister keen to reach her husband's home immediately requested him to see her off first. She did not want to get entangled between the two warring couple as well as be a party to any sinful act. He knew Aarti was head strong and once she made up her mind she would go ahead with her cause.

At his sister's he got delayed in formalities being conducted by her in laws. He excused himself prudently and retraced his steps quickly to the hospital. He asked for Aarti but they informed him that no lady with this name was being wheeled into the OT today. She had wisely enough supplied them with a false name. But as luck would have it just as she was being wheeled out of the theatre in semi-conscious state he set his eyes on her. Oh what *tamasha* he created right there at the corridors. He was no less a dramatic than her but a bad one she supplemented. When none of the staff, visitors, patients and their attendants took his antics seriously, he stepped out.

Hurriedly he ventured home and soon enough a big gathering of members of the joint family descended at the hospital. Compensation said some court-case said another divorce said one disallow her from the community devised another. As many heads as many talks ringed along the passage. Luckily for her the doctors had by then left for their homes in the premise. Before word could reach them she summoned all her relations near and admonished them strictly, if you want your peace do not utter a word. If you profess you are my family they shall charge you with the hefty bill and also negligence on the part of the family. While right now they are convinced of my plight so go along with my version of the account without any variation.

When the doctor arrived the now so called foster family backed off as suggested. When he asked her it seems these people who have flocked in here unannounced were saying they are your in-laws and family and created so much drama and dilemma such that we doctors were beckoned. They even ventured to say they would defame the hospital? Who are these people what do you have to say now he growled.

Aarti did some fast thinking and uttered doctor saab these are my neighbours and I consider them my family. So I describe them as my parents and they treat me as their daughter. My original family is in the remote village. This man here says he is your husband, demanded the doctor. My husband she feigned surprise, no no doctor saab he is my husband's younger brother these people rounded him off from his job and made him appear as my husband. Ask these people yourself and they shall tell you that that forsaken fellow my husband must be lying drunk somewhere she lied skilfully.

Now that I had achieved what I set out to I did not mind placating their ruffled feathers. Silly people she considered them, foolish of them to take my words verbatim. These people shall never rise above their present conditions for they fail to apply their minds.

Her daughter Rinki was married off with great show of pomp and grandeur. The marriage was the talk of the neighbourhood for weeks to come. I was again with the Bengali family in Delhi by then. She who had spent money like water, running from one hospital to the other with me when Rinki was afflicted and the doctor's had given up she was present at her wedding. I was not like this then I was as obese as a hippopotamus. I could not even bend to touch my daughter's feet during the ceremony.

The water of Kanpur is such that life there is regularly and intermittently dotted with sorrow. Forget my family I have seen affluence dwindle to penury. That is why I say that I shall never go back there. The city has not enough to offer. I hear it's going to be a smart city and plenty of schemes have been promulgated by simultaneous governments. Let's see but as of now I have no intentions, Dilli is my *karambhoomi* my bureau.

The same fate as Babli struck Rinki. She was back with me with a son and expecting another. I cooked for her gave her love and comfort I cajoled and coaxed her out of her plight. But inwardly I was fearful. I did not know the city well, did not have any relatives around, and did not know the hospitals. I had not ventured much. I was with a different employer.

But I am blessed to have favourable families as my employers. They have sided with me during all my turmoil's. It was at this time I was introduced to you. Your mother 'nani' was sick and you needed someone to look after her. I needed the money. Who was god sent for whom I do not know? The phase eased out comfortably guided by all. Nani knitted such colourful sweaters and lowers for my grandchildren. She blessed us profusely too. My daughter was overjoyed.

The child was born in Safdarjung hospital. The *kanhiyya*, he was named by the nurses, for only one male was born that day. In time Nani went back so did she to her husband later, to the cities they belong to.

Throughout the time Rinki was home Bengali was to remain hostile towards her. He resented her and the money spent on her. He appeared lost in thought. I was busy with the infant in the hospital. With great fanfare I was to bring him home. The day turned out to turn my world topsy-turvy. Bengali's phone had the facility to record his conversations, unknown to us. That day the recordings were detected by chance. I was livid I wished to burn the world down. But for the sake of children I went along.

My Bengali was seeing a woman. He who was so docile so dedicated had learnt the ways of the big bad city Delhi. Every now and then he would plead sorry and time and again he would revert. The day I decided to end all, my mind reeling under suspicion, I got a call from you. Are you coming today? The words shrugged me out of my misery. I was reporting absent for the past few days. I came and suddenly before I knew I was crying. I poured my grief my sorrow you listened and held me close in your arms. I was healed at that instance. You put everything in the right perceptive for me.

She was not one to take things lying down. She may have been bogged down by the suddenness. But she fought tooth and nail with his parents. She, who held on to decorum to never slight his name, declared war. She wore a burka and followed him. She stood listening to him at his workplace unknown to him. She gave money to the adjacent shop salesman to inform her about his movements. She began visiting him on pretexts. She had transformed from Durga to Kaali.

The Bengali family had wished to take me along. Before their retirement they took me to Kolkata with them. But I could not fancy the city, she tells. Firstly no one spoke Hindi there, then the fish smell was overbearing, then there was so much population on one hand and poverty around on

the other. Frankly, I could not foresee myself there. If the
child was to be born in Delhi how could I have gone there?
Though the joy of birth was short lived, I realised that had it
not been for the child the truth would never have surfaced.
The child is a blessing. The cheer was back. The trust is lost
it's my work that has remained faithful to me.

Have you been to any other city I ask? Yes she confirms.
With the Marwari family I have been to Ranchi. What
about Ranchi I ask? See, it happened like this. Jia told me
to inform my parents that tomorrow we shall go to Ranchi
and to get some cloths along. I thought like Green Park
or Phoolbag this was also a local campus, I was not aware
of. We went to the station we sat in the train and we kept
moving and moving. By evening I enquired when shall we
reach? Oh the next day I was told. I began to cry, alerted
Jia asked what happened. I told them I had not informed
my parents and they shall be worried by now. They pacified
me and the first thing they did on reaching was to call and
inform them that I was safe in their custody.

The city had dark hefty men with only eyes and mouth
visible. The soil was reddish. They spoke a different language.
Some relative of Jia's was ill. When I went to the market I
did not want to show that I could not understand them. I
would give them a hundred rupees note. Then on return do
some reverse math, that if he tended this amount then the
item cost was that much. One relative called me 'nonsense'
standing behind my back. I knew he was saying something
rude and conjured it meant some rubbish I confronted him
how dare you call me 'nonsense', tell me? He immediately
went 'sorry sorry'. Later he asked Jia is she educated, oh no
she does not even know how to read or write. He was in for
a great shock.

The hospital was a maze. You climbed up, but when you climbed down there was no exit. Again I would climb up everything was fine and again when I went down there was no exit. I was young then and felt so nervous, but then applied my mind; I went up again and followed the people going down. I was out in the open. She was talking of the basement, a concept she was unaware of, but what presence of mind one can but appreciate her.

I have been to Jhumritalaiya as well and to Allahabad and Mumbai too, to cook at weddings, this job is called *Sahalak* she enlightens. But I have not seen these cities. At Mumbai I did ask to be taken to the *Jheel* but we were staying far away from the sea. I came to know that Cinestars were not treated as vip here, they could be found roaming the streets. So I would sip my tea on the terrace and lookout in search for some Hero-Heroine. That is when I was informed that they roam in cars with tinted glass.

In my life I have lived righteous and on my terms. If I have been unsuccessful in some endeavours it's my family who has never left an opportunity to let me down. For just as she was coming to terms with adulterousness, her younger daughter put her into the eye of another storm? It was nearly two years since she had submitted herself and gone through a court marriage, she confided. Aarti befriended her. When she got to know of the extent of her relationship and their endurance she relented.

For her daughter, unknown to her was like her. She was adamant, her initial claim that she would leave her home only on getting parental approval had over the couple of years diluted its stance and now narrowed down to her mother's agreement only, based on her father's recent developments and track record. Needless to say Aarti was reminded of her parents and their disapproval. Practicality thy name could well be Aarti.

She who was the most stubborn obstacle in their path became their ally. She found herself in solitude again. The family disapproved of the alliance, its blasphemy they stomped in solidarity. The world stood against her but our solitary trooper trudged on. She sent her daughter Baatu to Kanpur on the pretext that Delhi is scorching hot.

She was making a lot of calls, Bengali was alarmed, he knew that once she had made up her mind she would be as obstinate as a disgruntle ox. They needed to know her plans. One night he literally seduced her, she blurted out her apprehensions and her arrangements for her daughter. He alarmed the family. Her son became her most ferocious foe. It seems Bengali was getting alarmed too often.

How obstinate can you be? Very she informs. Example I insist. Once, we were on vacation, at Kanpur. The whole family stood against me. Adamantly I darted and left home. Wandered by the day and took the evening train. When I reached Delhi I knew my neighbours would have been alarmed by Bengali and they would call and tell him of my whereabouts.

When I disembarked at the station there were a lot of families stranded there. There had been some mishap in Bihar, all trains were cancelled. Quickly I changed my mind and stayed at the platform with the ladies. How did you manage I wonder. You shall be surprised to know that one gets everything on the station. Food soap pillow water fan toilet facility, everything you name. Bengali was very alarmed he searched for me everywhere. The next day he even checked the papers for some unfortunate news. He also visited the mortuary.

Slowly and one by one she began garnering her foot soldiers her infantry her cavalry and finally her artillery. She leaves for Kanpur on the pretext of celebrating her grandson's first birthday. Alone she has carefully selected the trousseau, including maroon and gold bangles along with the traditional black.

She rues that Bengali and her son have not been able to find a match for her daughter in time. When they protest she says can you guarantee her future. Should the girl be married to someone else and were to abscond later to her paramour, would that not be more disgraceful and a total waste of expenditure. With age the spend-thrift attribute is being substituted by spend-tact.

At times her daughter and the boy who grew up calling Aarti 'sister' insist what the need for all this hype and celebrations is. She asserts it's a must required show of pageantry. For I want society to assert and give its stamp of permission and respectability to the both of you and your union. If there is any tinge of taint I want to carry it on my forehead. I want everyone to know what a mother can do for her daughter to see her future happy. For the daughter, who gave her so much respect by not stepping out of her threshold?

Bengali continues to side with her when he listens to her talk, then sides with the family when he listens to the family talk. Go ahead he once assured Aarti I'm behind you. Aarti insists for once be by my side or ahead of me, lead. But he has not the calibre of one who can lead. A leader is a person who can persuade people to accomplish a purpose impressively and imposingly.

I shall wait for that phone call to inform me that all has been well that the family relented. I know on her return she will say there was a time when I was about to lose all, the nature of life is to be in distress alone, now all is good.

Unknown to Aarti the real drama-production began on the night of 4th when some assailants ransacked and demolished the household items she had painstakingly amassed for her daughter in the house they rented.

She was incensed. All intelligence was being compromised. Only one counsel saw her through, that of propagating a deferred date for the ceremony and advancing the actual date of the commencement of the ritual. So while 9th was promulgated and publicized the marriage was solemnised on the 5th morning. Conducted in Arya Samaj fashion without any fuss where only few formalities of booking the temple for registering and conducting the marriage and submission of some documents are required. The fire is lit and the marriage conducted around it. The marriage certificate is then issued.

As per tradition in her family Baatu was given her farewell after the ceremony the fun-games lunch and merriment were over. She left with her husband carrying the *kalash* over which the lamp was lighted. This lamp is believed to defuse on its own. By then her opposing family got to know of the marriage being accomplished, their bane and base instincts came to the fore. They congregate in hordes at the rented house. Though, those planning to waylay her were in for the surprise themselves that led them to rubbing their hands in complete disappointment and dismay when they learnt of the marriage conducted with élan, they did not relent they retaliated in full form and fury. One furious kick and the sacred lamp feverishly furled to disintegrate. The oil spilled over Aarti's feet the patches still visible. When she got to know of the dilapidated and the rundown home, her heart sank vandalized.

Their exchange would heat up then flare up and then turn highly Rabelaisian. No one was spared they brought out the linen from the past generations to be presented to the present with risqué. If despite of this escapade by him and that misdemeanour by her, marriages are being conducted in the family they shall be performed henceforth too she hollered grotesquely at the barbs aimed at her. For once she was glad Bengali was not there as it amounted to one opponent less.

Aarti was prepared for war but what was unfolding before her was alien. It was gorilla war. There were traitor's infiltrators dictator's orators and some jesters too, how can a creation be complete without the comic? Bengali held his post at Delhi as told, he refused to budge when call after call were made to infuse him in the embargo and imbroglio. He was reminded of the day when one morning he was out.

A thief ran past him and on hearing the crowd follow he began running too in fright. He was caught. Aarti was cooking lunch when she got the news that Bengali was in police custody. She was told that he was an accomplice. Look at him does he look like one she thundered. He is innocent let him go. No they said not today. Today she persisted. He did not know the ways of the station but she did. By tomorrow he could be implicated in some case.

Today sir you leave him today she demanded. No way, he declared. If he was a culprit I would have brought him to you, he is innocent as a baby, kindly let him off or else she trailed off. Or else what he persisted? Or else you shall not remain on your seat too. If a woman harassed comes to being herself no one can match her. It might take you two minutes to remove your uniform but just a second for me to undress and shout, she said standing abreast and removing her sari *aanchal* for effect. Bengali was released then and there. He knew her calibre and competence.

None were going to give in so easily. Family honour pride reputation tradition *parampara* and many such lofty words were hurled. Her daughter was shut in a room. A sling match ensued. Volatility and randomness ruled the roost. That is when Aarti descended to her form. Verbal and physical tussle ensued. She caught the brick and the thick stick being hurled at them midway bruising her palm. She manifested into the vehement and the one raging with ferocity. She felt torn between her daughter and warring son.

Baatu too was tormented, she was asked to sign some papers to null and void the marriage. She relented when Aarti gave her the signal. Just one thought prevailed in her mind, somehow and anyhow she had to free her daughter from bondage. She did not board the train at the station. She saw the train in the yard from the bridge and they alighted and made their way to the train. The whole family was languishing at the railway station ready to pounce on sight. By the time they realised their folly they were northward bound.

While all the time she was furious and infuriated with Bengali and vowed to chuck him out on her return. When he got to know of it he was predictably alarmed. His mobile phone that was the curse of his troubles came to his rescue. He played the recordings for her before she could say anything. He was on her side threatening all, should any harm come to his daughter or wife.

Her sister in law's husband who was in constant touch with her and pledging alliance was the *ghar ka bhedi Lanka dhayey* meaning the insider who tried to bring about the fall of the mighty city Lanka. She was no Ravana to abduct she was one to solemnize and sanctify. The act 'the kick' was akin to the demons transcending to disrupt the consecrated fire. She took on the ravaging like the pious take on the demons who wandered in search of the saintly performing prayers and offerings to the sacred fire at the *vedi* the altar.

It is believed that during the *Tretayug* or the era when the Ramayana occurred there were two prevailing civilizations, the Arya and *Raakshash* or the demonic. Followers of the Arya meaning the noble and the respectable came to be known as the Aryan, the race that includes the Indo- Europeans. Whereas Arya Samaj the Hindu reform movement was founded by the religious leader Maharshi Dayanand Saraswati. He denounced ritual and idol worshipping and favoured the Vedic way. He advocated equal respect and equal rights for women. If he were to witness the above he would have been extremely proud of the Aarti's of today. *Shabash* to them bravo we hail them.

Had it not been her immediate family she would have called for the police to report the matter. But better sense prevailed. She took the newlywed to Etawah, she went to her old patrons and settled them in a new job at the rice mill and new home. She brought them with her so they could be with her and Bengali for a few days.

Her family too on the other hand went from one advocate to the other to check if any law by-law clause would favour them, when none were available they relented defeated. Aarti heaved a sigh of relief after sleepless months of anguish a glimmer of elation seeped into her being on my terms and conditions she sighed to herself. Afraid that if spoken audibly they may disrupt the house of cards she painstakingly assembles. It shall take her months if not years to know and realize for sure that her labour is rewarded by the concrete and not the cards she presumes.

It is Bengali she worries for now. For he says they cannot tell us not to come to Kanpur and sever ties at their wish. Like the previous year's this Diwali he wishes to prove a point to all by going.

When I walked out of my married home it was Ram-rajya time – the time when all is well and everything is right says Aarti. We just walked out. We needed to work hard we needed to send children to school. We needed to live appropriately. We would collect the dry laburnum fruits for cooking. We placed two bricks to fashion the makeshift stove. When we could not cook we mixed flour and water and fed the children, we would touch their feet to excuse us for we could not provide. We provided them with milk when we could afford. We started a vegetable shop the earnings was aplenty.

When the officers went on transfer or retired they chucked out a lot of things. We would get the discarded rack the chair the bowls the tray. They appeared so expensive then.

Bengali worked in the printing press but it was far off and soon he left it. The children were enrolled in school. We were growing vegetables in the abandoned back yard. Again I was stitching the sari falls, while Bengali would hem the edges. We were using the kerosene stove now; collecting fire wood was a task of the past. Bengali would cook for us. I look up a little startled, that is why I say he is the best he has always stood by me encouragingly.

I purchased the Tv along with the trolley. I made new friends. Though I do not understand English I liked watching their serials and films she informs with glee. When I look up at her she immediately corrects, in my last birth I was definitely born with rich trappings and fortune, wonder what wrongs I did that though the inherent attitude remains I have to work and slog as fated. We began going out for movies. I opened my first account in the bank. We worked at a hellish pace we slogged. We admitted our children to better schools.

We celebrated birthdays. I remember the day my son was unwell, I was in search of work. I have at that time slogged at the construction sites. What did you do? I would polish the stones, and it was a laborious task. If my family got to know they would discard me so I told them I have a job at the school. I would change into old clothes there and then transform again after the work was done. Bengali got to know of it, I pleaded with him to keep it a secret, we needed the money. It was good earning it was a job that paid me daily wages. I needed the money daily for the medicines for the foodstuff.

We were at my brother's place and someone commented that look at Aarti's palms they appear so gruff and worn. Bengali is a simple man he blurted out the truth. My brother's were appalled. When I was asked to put *alta* the red paint on women's feet at the Etawah marriage I agreed. Wonder of wonders each woman would get her feet painted in two minutes and then offer me twenty or forty or fifty rupees. That was the custom. More than all the revelry I was brimming with joy in my heart and adding up the amount. Oh its four hundred its five hundred I called up the ladies sister come and get your feet painted eight odd hundred I amassed.

When my brothers learnt of it they were dismayed. These jobs are below you they admonished. I told them I can leave them but not my work. Was that not what mother taught us I ask. They do not seem to remember. Work is my worship, working has become an obsession with me. Bengali is worried sometimes and sometimes in fun he teases me, wonder you shall someday go crazy working so much.

With money came party time. She always loved to share her happiness. She would cook some she would order some, food. And if she could manage a bottle of rum, bliss. She loves to be at the centre of attention to swing sway jive. She lives on her terms.

Again my cooking skills were recognised; every Holi- Diwali there was huge demand for me. Every person is a reluctant cook while I am the ready one, she claims prudently and righteously. It's her forte, it's her calling. We were destined to meet one day, she quips, I do not deny.

Ups downs and gossip are part and parcel of life. Things should not go out of proportion she believed for then it was time to act. She is grateful to each of her employer's. Without their benign blessings support and encouragement

I could not have come this far. I am happy very happy for 2015 has fulfilled all my aspirations. My story, which was an innermost desire of mine has been written is complete. God has been kind.

Working was her pride, she never tired of it. She began working for her children leaving her home and hearth. She worked as construction worker as an envelope and packet maker I can do all sorts of labour she claims there is none that she has not tried her hands at. Only one thing eludes me, education. There are times when I feel I should have focused on my lessons times when I have had to rely on others to tell me what is written. When I remember something that needs to be told to you I feel handicapped. By the grace of god I have good memory but wouldn't it be nicer if I could jot the thoughts down on paper as they occurred, she wonders aloud.

You do not need any of that, your memory has retained each word each incident each chapter as they occurred. You are a cut above the rest that is imported. When I recount something I have written she is charmed. You are good in science she tells me. And you I question for I know she is waiting for me ask the same to her. I always indulge her. Her answer leaves me totally flabbergasted, I can add divide subtract so she concludes I am good at math. It's like someone telling Mr Amitabh Bachchan, I am good at acting.

One day suddenly she remembered that though Bengali her husband was not the eldest son he was married before his elder brother for he was getting attracted to a neighbour's daughter Rekha. Hence it was decided that he be married off at the earliest, hence the rush to get him married before he smartens and gets sufficiently smitten. The middleman took advantage of this piece of information and acted accordingly, under the impression that once she gets a worthy daughter in law his mother would forgo and forget the value of cash. So that was the core reason for all the lives ups and downs she underwent and endured with her chin up since Bengali was with her throughout the journey. It's been an interesting life.

Tell me some more I persist. She divulges that the other day I asked him to get mutton. He did not get it. When I asked him why he said what is all this at this age you want to eat mutton. *Hurrr* I warn him my age is fine you may be aging but not me. He looks at the colourful cloths I wish to wear for Baatu's marriage and sighs, at this age, again I warn him, this is nothing, let me furnish and finish with my parental responsibility then see my colour's. What... what he stammers and enquires alarmed? I'll wear jeans and tee-shirt and roam the world. He knows and says that I always do what I say and I can be very stubborn too. Then he folds his hands and brings them to his forehead and says *nangai ke samne sab hare hain*, all are defeated when faced with one, hell-bent. He knows her best.

This piece of narration came my way out of context and I am also sharing it with the reader out of sequence. For it merited mention. Marriages shall continue to be made in heaven one may find fault put blame fix responsibility, but making the marriage a haven or heaven shall lie with the woman and the man. Magnanimity shall prevail petty shall perish.

She still searches for and flips Tv channels for Rekha films. When she could not recollect one particular song, I ask her for the details of the film and the song. I search and find the song from the film Aalap for her. I show it to her on my laptop. She is delighted and considers me very resourceful. I watch the song and can see why it has impacted her heart and mind and casted a lasting image on her. It's the song it's the toe-ring it's the bindi its the maroon-red bangles she wears it's her *sindoor* covered hair parting it's the way she wears her hair, it's the thought of domesticity of family. It's every single girls dream. The song she prefers most is... *kahe manwa naache humra sakhi re koi isse ab samjhaye.* https://www.youtube.com/watch?v=VFJ4zw2LjGY

A film directed by the renowned director Hrishikesh Mukherjee. Released in the year 1977.

In a straight and direct defiance to the proverbs by the Anonymous's and *Agyaat's* of the world the second class pass most probably in second division for she absconded school and classroom so often, her life was a living declaration of the fact that wisdom comes knowledge may linger.

I conduct a rapid fire contest

Happiest - at Kanpur Cantt.

Like - fashion

Hate - lies and deceit

Movie - all Amitabh Bachchan and Rekha starrer*

---

* Amithabh Bachchan was involved in an accident during Coolie picture, then I kept five *shukar/* friday fasts for him, she informs on the day I am wrapping up the tale and the loose ends.

Love - I love those who love me and those who don't love me I also do not love them. Rest is all pretence. The love that has endured is my love for cooking. Even if someone says at two in the night to cook I shall do it keenly.

Life - life is doing one's *karam* (work) and receiving the rewards. Don't stop earning money without it life is not happy.

Work - work is equivalent to money. It helps me to provide for my children to fulfil my dreams and that is how it keeps me happy. I do not have to fake-praise Bengali or my son in lieu of money.

Enjoy - eating out. I went to Gurgoan with my Bengali employer we had to pay toll to reach this place. It had kiosks and small light bulb decorations. There was a waterfall on one side, but I have a husband who does not like eating out.

Colour - maroon. For bindi for nailpaint

Dream- to run my own dhaba.

It shall happen soon I tell her and turn away, I know she is watching my back. We are like soul sisters. She has ruminated reflected recollected her life with me. If I ever have a secret I might just as well share it with her. If I ever want any worldly-wise advice I might just ask her. And when she opens her Dhaba I'll be the happiest and have a feast. Think she owes me a meal.

Women and water are comparable to each other in nature. When temperatures soar both are known to swell, one in volume the other in rage fury or irritation, the degrees shall decide the temperament on display. Like quicksilver one can evaporate without a trace while the other can show symptoms of ferociousness and fierceness evaporate at will, without any sound in both the cases. In wintry weather it is known to absorb all the chillness till it itself is freezing so does a women take all harshness on her own self till she is cold with fraught and frigid say some. It can rise upwards and uplift, to reach up to the heavens but its inherent characteristic is to remain the lowest denominator, to be grounded nurturing the roots, so it shower down as rain as affection. Women too are crafted to make the home they are contained into their identity, as does the liquid by acquiring the shape of its container. Spoil it and aqua turns dirty so does a women. Give it colour and both take the sheen of that presented mingling with the new adaptable to transform. If unheeded and if need be they can spill as in the case of water or spill the beans in the case of the feminine. Similar to the spirit of water they always find their levelheadedness. They are both transparent. Wonder of wonderments is that they can both exist in all of the three stages, solid liquid and vaporous. For women are known to be known as rock solid, are effortless to blend in any situation, a blender's pride so to say, and can illustrate being very sublime with an ethereal quality about them. Water has a density of 999.9 kg/ meter cube. Women are pure 24 carat till they are amalgamated with the impure for commercial or embellishment or enhancement or enrichment benefits and purposes. They feel advantaged when left free flowing but stagnate on storing up. Both water and women need preservation in our society, a civilization country city society community or individual that remains unaware and is the cause of their decline shall eventually decline and perish. That is the dictum. Even the Vedas pronounce that where women are not revered prosperity and wealth shall refuse to exist.

She was an outlier.

She feels liberated after the recent chaotic.

Now for the promised address

Aarti Shrivastava
(the cook)

12/1 Khedapati Mandir
Kanpur

Aarti why did you not go to school amused rued cajoled queried hinted all of her employers unanimously? In a way it was good that she did not. For else she would have ended up being one in the millions milling around and not the extraordinary heroine of our story, leading with genuine and generous aplomb her life on her terms and definitely on her conditions. She has come a long way.